THE WAFFEN-SS IN NORMANDY
JUNE 1944, THE CAEN SECTOR

CASEMATE | ILLUSTRATED

CASEMATE | ILLUSTRATED

THE WAFFEN-SS IN NORMANDY

JUNE 1944, THE CAEN SECTOR

YVES BUFFETAUT

CASEMATE | ILLUSTRATED

MILITARIA

CIS0003

Print Edition: ISBN 978-1-61200-6055
Digital Edition: ISBN 978-1-61200-6062

This book is published in cooperation with and under license from Histoire & Collections. Originally published in French as Militaria Hors-Serie No 87, © Histoire & Collections 2013

Translation by Myriam Bell
Design by Paul Hewitt, Battlefield Design
Color artwork by Jean Restayn © Histoire & Collections
Original cartography by Sandra Gosselin
Photo retouching and separations by Remy Spezzano
Additional text by Steve Smith and Ruth Sheppard
Printed and bound by Megaprint, Turkey

CASEMATE PUBLISHERS (US)
Telephone (610) 853-9131
Fax (610) 853-9146
Email: casemate@casematepublishers.com
www.casematepublishers.com

CASEMATE PUBLISHERS (UK)
Telephone (01865) 241249
Fax (01865) 794449
Email: casemate-uk@casematepublishers.co.uk
www.casematepublishers.co.uk

Title page image: A close-up shot of a Tiger, showing the details of the Zimmerit, and the insignia of I SS Panzer Corps. (© through Jean Restayn)
Contents page images: Map of Normandy 13–30 June 1944. (Department of History at the United States Military Academy)
A Panzer IV from 9th SS Panzer Regiment that has been well camouflaged in the bocage of Normandy. (© through Jean Restayn)

Please note: armored vehicles and vehicles illustrations are not to scale.

Contents

Timeline of Events 6

The Waffen-SS in 1944 8

The SS Divisions in Normandy 24

First Battles of the Hitlerjugend 52

The Desert Rats and a Tiger 99

Operation *Epsom* 120

Afterword 124

Further Reading 125

Index 126

Timeline of Events

In June 1944 there were some 55 German divisions in France and the Low Countries. In northwest France, the Fifteenth Army was defending the area around Calais, and the Seventh Army was stationed near Normandy. While the Germans expected the Allies to attempt an invasion, successful Allied deception indicated that the location of such a landing would be Calais. Once the landings in Normandy began, the Germans had to not only try to contain the invasion with the forces in position, but also urgently bring forward more divisions from the interior.

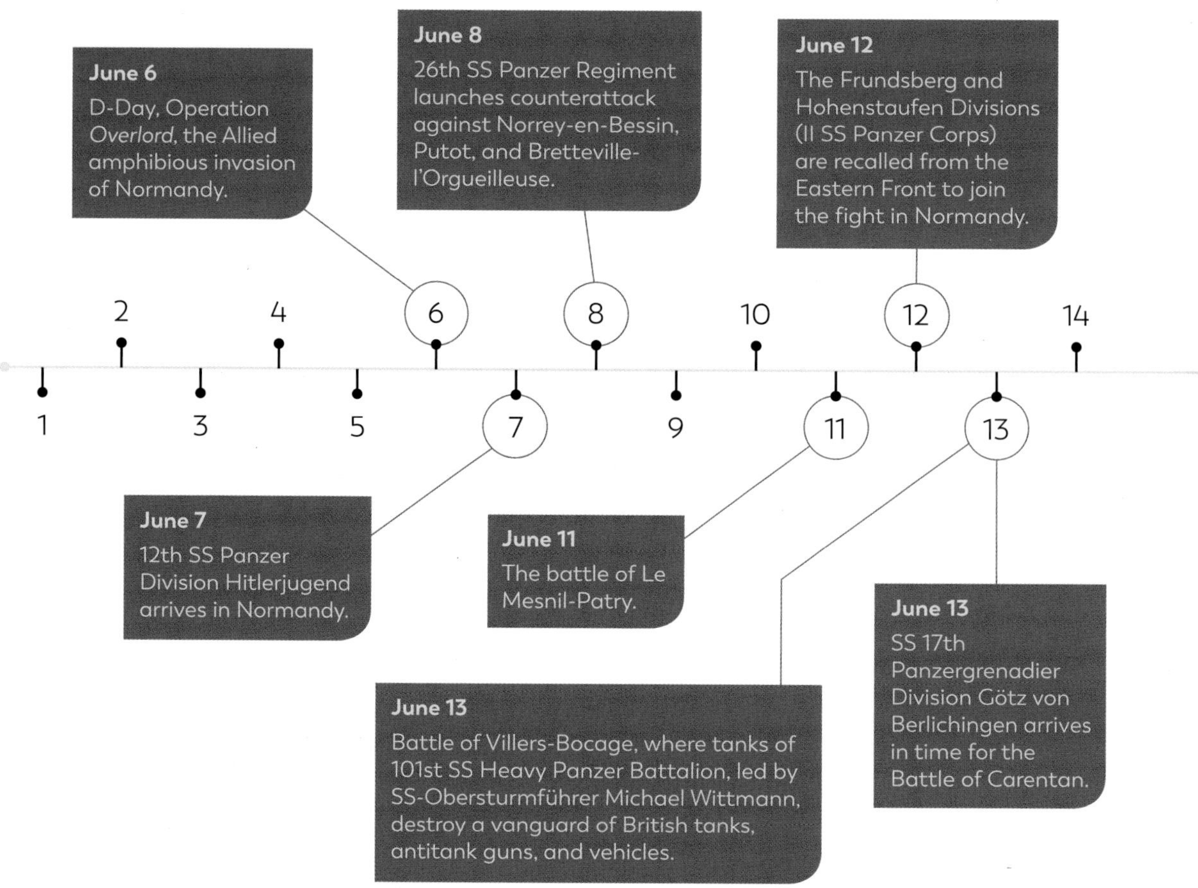

Panther no. 318, 1st SS Panzer Regiment, Leibstandarte SS Adolf Hitler. (© Jean Restayn)

June 19
A massive storm blows onto the beaches, causing Allied delays and grounding their airpower for three days.

June 25
British XXX Corps attempts to drive a wedge into the left flank of SS Hitlerjugend.

June 26
The British launch Operation *Epsom*, intended to cut off German-held Caen.

June 28
1st SS Panzer Division Leibstandarte Adolf Hitler begins to arrive at the front.

June 30
II SS Panzer Corps arrives, counterattacks British VIII Corps, and causes Montgomery to shut down Operation *Epsom*.

The Waffen-SS in 1944

It has been argued that the men of the Waffen-SS represented the archetypal warrior in World War II: well-armed and trained, with well-honed fighting skills, and accustomed to taking the lead in the most difficult battles. Also imbued with political ideology, a soldier of the Waffen-SS was expected to be the ultimate elite soldier. But by the time of the Allied invasion of Normandy on D-Day, was this depiction of the Waffen-SS still accurate? Or had it become a myth, with the earlier reputation of the Waffen-SS exceeding the actual reality? Indeed, opinions on the Waffen-SS units that fought during the Battle of Normandy vary, not only among today's historians, but also among contemporary German generals.

To answer this question we can start with an evaluation of the German panzer divisions that was not a judgment made by the Allies but by a senior German commander at the time, in the Geyr von Schweppenburg report. A seasoned battlefield general, von Schweppenburg

A Pak 40 from 12th SS Panzer Division Hitlerjugend, in position in the hedgerows of Normandy, during the fight of June 1944. (© through Jean Restayn)

Some very young soldiers from the 12th SS Panzer Division, having fun with a veteran old enough to be their father. (© through Jean Restayn)

was commander of Panzer Group West, a training and tactical headquarters designed to ensure a full-fledged armored reserve to respond to an Allied invasion; and the light it sheds on the matter means we have to challenge many of our preconceived ideas.

The SS Divisions in June 1944 Were Not the Most Efficient

Because of the horrific fighting in Russia—particularly the spectacular counteroffensive of the SS Panzer Corps in the wake of Stalingrad, and its spearhead role at Kursk—there is a tendency to consider the SS divisions the elite of the German army. But this did not necessarily remain the case in Normandy. There are a number of reasons for this.

The first is that after the loss of so many officers in Russia, the Waffen-SS units suffered from a deficit in officers and non-commissioned officers (NCOs). Even though the SS divisions had priority in terms of the allocation of resources and new recruits, the lack of officers remained. After all, while new recruits could be found, they were ever younger and leadership skills had to be earned in the field, or at least provided through special training. This problem was exacerbated because Waffen-SS divisions contained more infantry (panzergrenadier) battalions than Heer (army) panzer divisions, and about twice as many as Allied armored divisions. Experience in Russia had taught the Waffen-SS to rely on their own integral infantry to fight alongside the tanks. (Infantry-tank coordination was a skill

A crew of 101st SS Heavy Panzer Battalion feeding a raven at the beginning of the Battle of Normandy. (© through Jean Restayn)

the Allies still had to learn painfully.) There was also the factor that Heer officers often did not want to join these highly politicized divisions. If an officer was seconded to the Waffen-SS he could not backtrack; returning to the Heer was not allowed.

Schweppenburg wrote: "The circle of officers and NCOs is rather small, and often of poor quality. A few losses or changes in the hierarchy of a division can lead to a great deterioration in the combat value. This value is largely due to the presence of some "characters." For instance, the 12th SS Panzer Division's performance relied on Fritz Witt (killed in action), on Kurt Meyer (his successor), and on a few battalion commanders." To this one could add that the young rank and file of the Hitlerjugend more than fulfilled the expectations of their commanders in Normandy, their first battle.

Schweppenburg also complained of the way what he calls the "Berchtesgaden staff"—that is the Oberkommando der Wehrmacht (OKW)—composed the strategic armored reserve available in France, which was to face the Normandy landings. It consisted of the 1st SS Panzer Division Leibstandarte Adolf Hitler; 12th SS Panzer Division Hitlerjugend; the Panzer Lehr Division; and 17th SS Panzergrenadier Division Götz von Berlichingen. Schweppenburg's personal preference would have been the following units: 2nd Panzer Division; 12th SS Panzer Division; 11th Panzer Division; 9th SS Panzer Division Hohenstaufen; and the Panzer Lehr.

Schweppenburg thought that the armored divisions' efficiency in 1944 was not more than 30 to 40 percent of what it had been in 1939. This verdict seems quite severe, but the

Panzer Group West commander had grounds for his reasoning. He compiled a list of the armored divisions available in the West, placing them into categories A to D, with A being the best:

A

- 2nd Panzer Division
- 9th SS Panzer Division
- 12th SS Panzer Division
- Panzer Lehr Division

B

- 11th Panzer Division
- 2nd SS Panzer Division
- 21st Panzer Division

C

- 9th Panzer Division
- 17th SS Panzergrenadier Division
- 116th Panzer Division

D

- 10th SS Panzer Division
- 1st SS Panzer Division

Soldiers of 25th SS Panzergrenadier Regiment, during the fights northwest of Caen. (© through Jean Restayn)

1st SS Panzer Division Leibstandarte Adolf Hitler arriving by train in the Paris sector on their way to the Normandy front. Seen here, a Flak on a Panzer 38 (t) of the 10th Flak, 1st SS Panzer Regiment. (Jean Restayn collection)

His categorization is rather surprising as it shows the 21st Panzer Division, with its motley French equipment, as more efficient than the 1st SS Panzer Division Leibstandarte Adolf Hitler. Then again, 21st Panzer—reconstituted after the original was lost in Tunisia in May 1943—had never fought in Russia, while the Leibstandarte had only been extricated after the near-destruction of 1st Panzer Army in mid-April 1944. It is useful to note that von Schweppenburg's classification was established before D-Day and does not take into account the performance of these divisions during the battle. However some of the comments he makes seem to take into account—at least partially—what was later learnt from D-Day.

Schweppenburg's Explanation for his Classification

2nd Panzer Division

The commanding officer [Heinrich von Lüttwitz] was a good leader on the ground, but less comfortable with training. The General Inspectorate has privileged the division in both staff and equipment. General Guderian used to be in charge of the division before the war.

9th SS Panzer Division

The division's performance depended on the remarkable personality of its commander, Obergruppenführer Bittrich, a first-class leader. The division was especially efficient against airborne operations (as proven at Arnhem) and in joint tank/infantry operations.

12th SS Panzer Division

The commanding officer [Fritz Witt, then Kurt Meyer] was efficient in training and possessed a strong will and passion for advanced combat techniques. The quality of recruits was good but the level of the subordinate officers and NCOs was mediocre.

Panzer Lehr Division

The division was well equipped by the General Inspectorate. The commanding officer [Fritz Bayerlein] had very modern thinking on training and combat techniques. There were however, deficiencies in infantry tactics and tank coordination.

11th Panzer Division

The commanding officer [Wend von Wietersheim] had a lot of experience in mobile warfare. The division had thus received high-quality training. It benefited from experienced officers and its recruits came from the 273rd Reserve Panzer Division.

Panther Ausf. G no. 219 of 1st SS Panzer Regiment Hitlerjugend.
(© through Jean Restayn)

2nd SS Panzer Division (Das Reich)

The division, which had just been reformed in France, still had a sufficient number of veterans from the time when it was first created by Paul Hausser, who had given it very high standards. The division had the best tank battalions in the West.

21st Panzer Division

The division had been reorganized after the African campaign, with undesirable personnel coming from a great many divisions. Despite intense and well-led training, this fault in the division was never overcome. Some of the equipment came from French factories.

9th Panzer Division

This division had undergone too many changes in its senior officers including the main staff officers. Furthermore, the training was disturbed by fortification building works.

A Panzer IV from 9th SS Panzer Regiment that has been well camouflaged in the bocage of Normandy. (© through Jean Restayn)

Erwin Rommel and Sepp Dietrich, the commanding officer of I SS Panzer Corps at the beginning of the Battle of Normandy. (© through Jean Restayn)

17th SS Panzergrenadier Division

Its performance rested mainly on the shoulders of two men, commander SS-Brigadeführer Werner Ostendorf, and SS-Standartenführer Jacob Fick, commander of the Panzergrenadier Regiment. It had poor equipment. The division organized and trained in a rush, showed itself quite able, but deteriorated quickly after Ostendorf was injured in Normandy.

10th SS Panzer Division

This division had poor luck in the choice of its commanding officers.

1st SS Panzer Division

The very definition of a praetorian guard, this division was bled white in Russia and never managed to make up for its losses, or for the fact that its officers were sent away to other divisions. (The 12th SS Panzer Division was created with officers from the 1st SS Panzer Division). Poor discipline, NCOs mediocre. The division had no time to train before D-Day.

Thus the famous Leibstandarte Adolf Hitler was just a second-rate division in Normandy, with failing discipline and average officers. Could this simply be the biased view of a Heer general officer? It would appear not, as it is corroborated in a report written by Günther Blumentritt, Chief of Staff to von Rundstedt's Oberbefehlshaber West (OB West).

A young recruit from the 12th SS Panzer Division refreshes himself during the fighting. His haircut is typical of this unit. (© through Jean Restayn)

A man from the 12th SS Panzer Division HitlerJugend adjusts the engine of an Opel car. The division's insignia is visible painted on the right wing of the vehicle. (© Jean Restayn collection)

Günther Blumentritt in 1944. (Bundesarchiv, Bild 101I-717-0010-03)

In profile: Günther Blumentritt

Günther Blumentritt joined the Prussian Army in 1911, and served on the Eastern Front during World War I. His experiences led him to develop a great respect for Russian soldiers. Between the wars he served as a staff officer. In 1939 he developed the plan for the invasion of Poland, *Fall Weiss*. In September 1939 he was made Chief of Operations for Army Group South, one of the armies that invaded Poland. In 1940, he was Operations Officer of Army Group A, and was part of the planning team for the invasion of France. Immediately after the Fall of France, he took part in the planning for the invasion of Great Britain, although he never believed it was a serious plan. Blumentritt was made Chief of Staff of Fourth Army just before the invasion of Russia—during the Russian counteroffensive, Fourth Army only narrowly escaped destruction outside Moscow. In 1942, Blumentritt was made Chief of Staff to von Rundstedt, who was overall commander of German forces in the West. He was responsible for much of the planning for the defense of France against invasion. He and von Rundstedt were surprised by the location of the Allied landings in June 1944—they had not expected landings on the Cherbourg peninsula and had not deployed strong forces there. Blumentritt remained in his position even after von Rundstedt was relieved of command. He was implicated in the July conspiracy to kill Hitler, but Hitler did not believe him guilty. Indeed he was later awarded the Knight's Cross. After the war he wrote several books, including *Von Rundstedt: The Soldier and the Man*.

This headquarters, directly subordinate to the OKW (German Armed Forces High Command), and so Hitler himself, managed the two major operational entities on the Western Front: Army Group B (Fifteenth Army, Seventh Army, and some units in the Netherlands) and Army Group G (First Army, Nineteenth Army and security forces in the Pyrenees). The Luftwaffe 3 and the Marine Group West only depended on the OB West for the tactical defense of the coast.

The chain of command was, however, particularly complicated. The Waffen-SS was under OB West orders from a tactical point of view only. For anything else it reported to Reichsführer SS Himmler, outranking the Heer, including Rommel and von Rundstedt.

In his report, written just after the war, Blumentritt noted that the OB West had no reserves of its own. The strategic reserve depended directly on Hitler, not von Rundstedt, and even less so on Rommel. The two army groups did have reserves, but more tactical than strategic: no decisive counterattack could be launched without the involvement of OKW Reserve.

This Panzer IV belongs to the 12th SS Panzer Division Hitlerjugend, as shown by the insignia painted on the right-hand mud-guard. (© through Jean Restayn)

A Panzer IV and a Panther in the background, during the Montauban maneuvers, May 1944. They belong to the 2nd SS Panzer Regiment, of the Das Reich Division. (© through Jean Restayn)

This reserve included three panzer divisions, two of which were SS: the 12th SS Panzer Division Hitlerjugend, and the 1st SS Panzer Division Leibstandarte Adolf Hitler. The third division was the Panzer Lehr. Once released by OKW, Panzer Group West would be activated as a tactical headquarters. However, these three divisions were quite dispersed at the time of the invasion—the 12th SS and the Panzer Lehr were roughly situated between Paris and Le Mans, while the Leibstandarte was located in Belgium.

When Blumentritt classified the 60 divisions potentially available to the OB West, he defined five categories:

- The armored divisions, including the SS divisions
- The fallschirmjäger (paratroop) divisions
- The standard infantry divisions
- The static coastal divisions
- The Luftwaffe field divisions. This last category was separate: the men were usually good, but their infantry training was lacking.

Blumentritt did not consider all the armored divisions to be of the same standard. The better two, from an equipment point of view, were the 2nd Panzer Division and the Panzer Lehr, which was logical, because 2nd Panzer had been pulled from the Eastern Front in October 1943, and Panzer Lehr was newly constituted (though laced with many veterans). This quashes the myth that SS units were always better equipped than Heer formations, as German production could not always keep up with severe losses. What about the men? According to Blumentritt:

> **The SS divisions' officers are less satisfactory [than those of the Heer]. In 1944, all the divisions have been employed in the East and the West. They have been re-organized several times and do not have the same value as the ones from 1939–40. Because of the fuel shortage, tank drivers do not receive sufficient training and consequently they do not drive well on all terrains, which causes numerous breakdowns.**

This is a fair statement. However, the longing of Blumentritt (and Geyr) for the unbloodied personnel of 1939–40 suggests a disservice to the newer classes of young men (born in 1926 and beyond) who grew up with the war, began training in rudimentary fashion while still boys, and who were eager to emulate the heroes they had heard about in service of their country. The majority of SS Hitlerjugend were only 18 years old at the time of D-Day, while the new personnel of 17th SS PzG, and even the reconstituted Leibstandarte, averaged under 20. In all cases, though, they were led by Eastern Front veterans, who knew the business of war well. An interesting recollection in this regard came from Kurt Meyer as he recalled the

These three young recruits from the No. 3 Zug, 15th Company, 25th SS Panzergrenadier Regiment, have just received the Iron Cross, Second Class in the Abbey of Ardenne, after the Mesnil-Patry fights. (© through Jean Restayn)

(US National Archives)

In profile:
Geyr von Schweppenburg

Leo Geyr von Schweppenburg joined the German army at the age of 18, in 1904. He served on several fronts during World War I, and remained in the army after the war. By 1937 he was a Generalleutenant in command of the 3rd Panzer Division. In the Poland campaign he was a divisional commander, and in February 1940 he was promoted to General der Kavallerie of XXIV Panzer Corps, which he commanded through the invasion of France. His corps was part of Guderian's Second Panzer Army during Operation *Barbarossa*, which led the advance towards Moscow. In late 1943 he was transferred from the Eastern Front to command Panzer Group West in northern France. Panzer Group West was the main force of armored units in northern France, the armored reserve for OB West. Rommel and Rundstedt disagreed as to how Panzer Group West would be employed against an Allied invasion, Geyr agreed with von Rundstedt that the panzer group should be held in reserve at a distance from the front. By June 8, Geyr had managed to move three panzer divisions north to protect Caen, and was planning a full-scale counterattack, but the following day his command post was destroyed by Allied air attack. Geyr was wounded and many of his officers were killed, forcing the cancellation of the counterattack. His units were able to slow the British advance for several weeks, but Geyr was relieved of command on July 2, after agreeing with von Rundstedt that there should be a strategic withdrawal from Caen. Geyr then served as an inspector general of armored troops until the end of the war. He died in 1974.

initial march of his Hitlerjugend 25th Panzergrenadiers to Normandy: "We, the old soldiers, face the future with anxiety. We sense what lies ahead. In comparison, the magnificent young grenadiers look at us with laughter in their eyes. They have no fear." It is also worth noting that the German panzers themselves had improved considerably by 1944. The upgunned Mark IVs and Panthers that comprised the Waffen-SS panzer regiments in Normandy would have been envied by the original personnel of 1939–40.

Before discussing the SS divisions' engagements on the invasion front, we will examine their exact composition. The figures for the divisions differ depending on the source.[1]

A 12th SS Panzer Regiment panzer, destroyed near Rauray on June 27, 1944. (© Imperial War Museum)

1 We have used in particular Thomas Jentz, *Panzertruppen* (Schiffer Military History, 1966) and Niklas Zetterling, *Normandy 1944: German Military Organization* (Fedorowicz Publishing, 2000).

The SS Divisions in Normandy

In all, six Waffen-SS divisions fought during the Battle of Normandy, as well as two Tiger tank battalions; however, due to the surprise of the invasion in both location and timing, their deployment had to be improvised and was by no means carefully planned. Apart from the II SS Panzer Corps, which transited from Poland to hit a crucial sector of the front at the end of June, the divisions arrived in a disordered fashion and were immediately thrown into the battle when they arrived. This usually meant recon units first, followed by panzergrenadiers, with tracked vehicles arriving later. Due to the lack of German infantry divisions at the front, the Waffen-SS units had to be plugged into the line in defensive roles. They could therefore never launch an effective counteroffensive. Only Operation *Lüttich*, launched in August through Mortain, saw a real concentration of panzers, but it came too late and with insufficient numbers.

A Panzer IV of 2nd Battalion, 12th SS Panzer Regiment, heading towards the front on June 6 or 7, 1944. The crew is smiling—the Germans, far from fearing the landings, welcomed them: it was the only way to defeat the British and Americans before forcefully turning on the Russians. (© ECPAD)

Tiger no. 223 of the SS Heavy Panzer Battalion, on the hill of Gournay-en-Bray, in the direction of Les Andelys. (© ECPAD)

The 12th SS Panzer Division Hitlerjugend was stationed closest and began to arrive first, on June 7, 1944 above Caen, with 17,000 men. Next was the reconnaissance battalion of the 17th SS Panzergrenadier Division Götz von Berlichingen, in the American sector, on June 9. The rest of this division was operational by June 13. The day before, the 101st SS Heavy Panzer Battalion had arrived in support of I SS Panzer Corps.

On June 28, over three weeks after the invasion there was the more orderly arrival of 1st SS Panzergrenadier Regiment, Leibstandarte Adolf Hitler. It was a vanguard element since the bulk of 1st SS Panzer Division only reached the front on July 4. During this time, lead elements of the 9th and 10th SS Panzer Divisions appeared in Normandy on June 29, as well as Kampfgruppe Weidinger, the vanguard of 2nd SS Panzer Division Das Reich. More of this division arrived on July 1, but some of its heavier, tracked elements only arrived on July 25.

The other Tiger battalion, 102nd SS Heavy Panzer Battalion, accompanied II SS Panzer Corps to the front on July 3. Thus, for over a month after the invasion, Waffen-SS units were still arriving incrementally, and then only after running a gauntlet of air attacks, with numerous rails and bridges destroyed. Meantime, Allied strength through the beaches had been increasing exponentially.

There was only one further element that reached the front later: the 17th SS Panzerjäger (Antitank) Battalion, which arrived on August 4. After that the only reinforcements that continued to arrive in Normandy up to August 15 were Heer units.

In Profile:
Half-tracks SDKFZ 250

An SdKfz 250 from the 3rd Company, 12th SS Panzer Reconnaissance Battalion.

The SdKfz 250 no. 312 from the 3rd Company, 12th SS Panzer Reconnaissance Battalion. It is armed with a MG42 with shield.

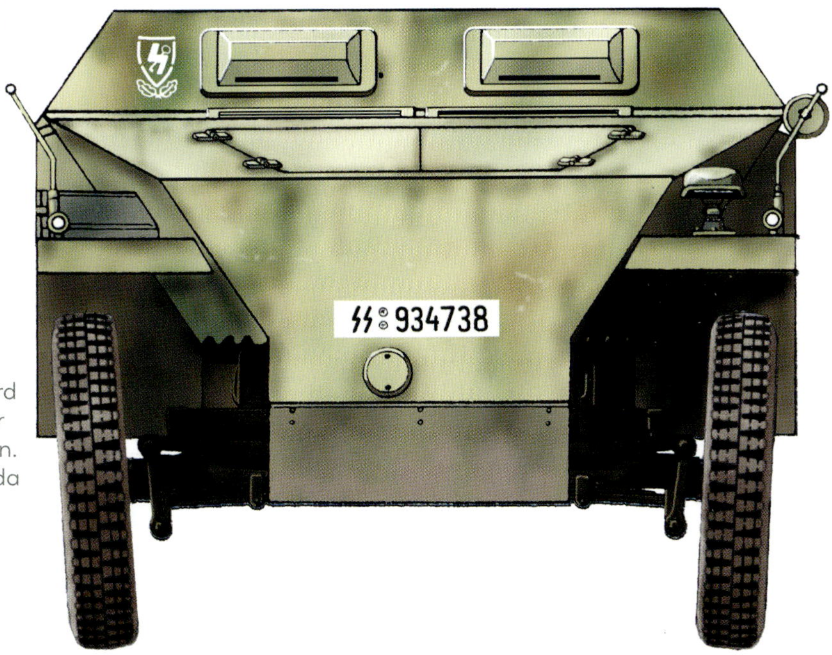

An SdKfz 250 from the 3rd Company, 12th SS Panzer Reconnaissance Battalion. It is equipped with a Breda light gun.

SS-Untersturmführer Thomas Amselgruber's Tiger no. 331 and crew, in Normandy. (© ECPAD)

In terms of numbers, the total of Waffen-SS men who fought in Normandy came to 96,754 men, not counting possible replacements during the battle. These are considerable numbers. Let us now take a look at the units' composition by numerical order, starting with the two heavy battalions, which were equipped with Tigers, the most formidable tank on either side.

101st SS Heavy Panzer Battalion

The 101st SS Heavy Panzer Battalion (s. SS Panzerabteilung 101) was created as part of I SS Panzer Corps, in Mailly-le-Camp on October 22, 1943, from a Tiger battalion.

On June 1, 1944 the battalion was situated near Beauvais, which allowed it to intervene promptly to the north or the south of the Seine if the need arose. At this time, the battalion had 37 operational Tigers and eight undergoing maintenance. The only reinforcements earmarked for the unit during the battle would be five Tiger IIs which left Germany on July 28, plus nine others that left on July 31 or August 1. Given the situation in France, it is not known whether these tanks got any further than Mailly-le-Camp.

The unit's first engagement was the famous battle of Villers-Bocage.

SS-Sturmbannführer Heinz von Westernhagen, commanding officer of 101st SS Heavy Panzer Battalion, wearing camouflage (facing the camera) and Hanno Rasch, commander of Tiger no. 311, wearing a motorcycle coat, during the maneuvers near Beauvais. (© ECPAD)

Aerial view of the bombardment of Caen, June 6, 1944. (U.S. Army)

In Profile: Caen

About 15 kilometers from the coast, the city of Caen sits astride the Orne River and the Caen canal and is the junction of several major roads. The Allied invasion plans required that the invaders quickly gain control of the major roads in Normandy and so it was imperative that Caen, Bayeux and Carentan be taken. The plan called for the British 3rd Infantry Division to capture the city by the end of June 6. On D-Day 3rd Infantry Division made good initial progress from Sword Beach towards Caen but was severely held up by a number of strongpoints. Other troops and tanks destined for the drive toward Caen were held up by traffic at the beachheads.

On June 9, Montgomery ordered a pincer attack to be launched against Caen, involving I Corps with the 51st (Highland) Infantry and XXX Corps. I Corps' attack was delayed until June 12; the 51st Highland Division did attack but 21st Panzer Division put up a determined defense and the offensive had to be called off. Meanwhile 7th Armoured Division was ordered to push into a gap in the German front towards Villers-Bocage (see page 109). After the battle of Villers-Bocage, the division was withdrawn on June 14. It would take several more offensives by British and Canadians and over another month of fighting before Caen was finally captured by the Allies. By that time much of the city had been completely destroyed by Allied bombing, and the civilian population had suffered greatly from both the bombing and ground combat.

View of Tiger no. 211 from the SS Heavy Panzer Battalion in Normandy. (© ECPAD)

Another view of Tiger no. 211 from the SS Heavy Panzer Battalion in Normandy. (© ECPAD)

102nd SS Heavy Panzer Battalion

This unit (s. SS Panzer Abteilung 102) was created at the same time as its sister battalion but was assigned to II SS Panzer Corps (9th and 10th SS Panzer).

At the beginning of June 1944, the 102nd SS Heavy Panzer Battalion was in Oldebroek, in the Netherlands. It was not operational as most of the drivers were training in Paderborn, Germany. The radio operators were not there either, nor were their 70 technicians. All would rejoin the unit quickly around June 15, but only to perfect their training. By this time, the battalion had its full quota of 45 Tigers and would not receive any more during the Battle of Normandy.

On June 22, departures toward Normandy began and would continue over several days. The tanks' arrivals at Versailles station only ended on July 2. The battalion arrived at the Normandy front a week later, and during the battle remained with II SS Panzer Corps, most often acting as a replacement for the missing Panther battalion of the 10th SS Panzer Division Frundsberg.

The 1st SS Panzer Division Leibstandarte Adolf Hitler

This flagship Waffen-SS formation fought from the start on the Eastern Front, earning great victories in 1943, though these came at a heavy price, both in equipment and in men. When the division was sent to Belgium to be reconstituted in April 1944, it was only a shadow of its former self.

The numbers for the unit on June 1, 1944 are misleading. Many men had been sent to reinforce it, increasing its ranks to 19,618 soldiers, but the majority of them were undertrained. Several thousand men had been transferred from the Luftwaffe or Kriegsmarine, and over two thousand from the then-overstrength Hitlerjugend. More than a thousand men were actually in Germany at that time in order to receive better training, including a lot of NCOs; but the quality of the troops had nothing on the soldiers of the previous years and the Leibstandarte Adolf Hitler of 1944 was an elite unit only on paper.

A Panzer IV from 7th Company, 1st SS Panzer Regiment, well camouflaged in the Forest of Cinglais, between Caen and Falaise. (Jean Restayn collection)

In Profile:
Medium Panzer IV Tanks

Panzer IV Ausf. H no. 622, 6th Company, 2nd Battalion, 2nd SS Panzer Regiment, Das Reich Division.

Panzer IV Ausf. H no. 614, 6th Company, 2nd Battalion, 10th SS Panzer Regiment, Frundsberg Division.

Panzer IV Ausf. H no. 514, 5th Company, 2nd Battalion, 9th SS Panzer Regiment, Hohenstaufen Division.

The motorized element had fared even worse, in part because when units transferred from the east they had to leave heavy equipment behind, counting on resupply from Germany: on June 1, 1944, while reforming in Belgium, the division didn't have a single armored half-track of the SdKfz 251 type, and of its 3,887 trucks, only 1,070 were in working order.

The number of tanks was equally woeful. On June 1, the division had 42 operational Panzer IVs, 38 Panthers and 44 StuG IIIs, with eight other Panzer IVs and one StuG in the repair shop. The standard figure of 98 Panzer IVs would eventually be reached in June with 33 Panzer IVs leaving Germany on June 8, and a further 20 on June 17. Meanwhile the Panthers were sent in smaller batches, from the factories, with six being sent from Germany on June 14, eight on the 17th, eight on the 18th, six on the 19th and finally six others on June 29.

The grand total was 103 Panzer IVs, 72 Panthers and 45 StuG IIIs. No reinforcements would arrive during the battle.

The division started to embark on trains heading for Normandy from June 17, arriving piecemeal. On June 25, 20 trains had been unloaded in Paris. In June, only one unit of the division was engaged on the front—the 1st SS Panzergrenadier Regiment, minus its 3rd battalion, which fought along the Nationale 175 Road south of Caen, during the British *Epsom* offensive.

Re-supplying 1st SS Panzer Division Leibstandarte Adolf Hitler, in the Forest of Cinglais. (Jean Restayn collection)

It was only from July 6 that the division was able to start fighting as intended, but its numbers still did not rise above 14,000 men, with 5,000 remaining in Belgium, waiting for their equipment and to complete training.

On July 1, some SdKfz 251s were finally delivered: 36 were operational, with 224 still requiring work. The number of trucks was 1,441 in working order and a further 613 in need of repair.

The first significant engagement of the division in Normandy was Operation *Goodwood* (July 18–20). Though at that time in reserve, the division was launched into battle to stop the British breakthrough, which it successfully did with the help of other German divisions.

The Leibstandarte artillery was disparate, including light field guns, heavy howitzers, 105mm guns, Wespes, Hummels, and Nebelwerfers.

As the division had been a late arrival, and had probably not lost more than 2,000 men in June and July, it was selected for the counterattack in Mortain, and moved out on the

Heinz Guderian talking with the commander of Leibstandarte Adolf Hitler, SS-Brigadeführer Heinz Lammerding, during the maneuvers in the Montauban region, in May 1944. (Jean Restayn collection)

Two Das Reich II StuG Battalion officers, Krag and Rheininshausen, with their mascot. (Jean Restayn collection)

night of August 5/6. After that calamity, during the following weeks the division managed to escape the Falaise pocket but, according to a report from Army Group B to the OB West, lost all its tanks and artillery there.

It is interesting to note that before Operation *Lüttich*, the Mortain counterattack, the division still had 57 Panzer IVs, 46 Panthers and 27 StuG IIIs in working order. At the end of it, on August 13, these numbers had fallen to 14 Panzer IVs, seven Panthers and eight StuG IIIs: 43 Panzer IVs were lost, as well as 39 Panthers, and 19 StuG IIIs.

The division's casualties for the duration of the battle fell between 5,000 and 6,000 killed, wounded, missing and captured.

The 2nd SS Panzer Division Das Reich

The Das Reich Division originated before the outbreak of World War II (as the Verfügungstruppe) and had, in different forms, taken part in all the major campaigns of the war: Poland, France, Yugoslavia, and Russia. After it became a panzergrenadier division, it showed its worth during the battle of Kharkov in the spring of 1943, then at Kursk. Obviously these battles were costly and by December 1, 1943, there were almost 8,000 men missing from the division.

At the end of that month, the Das Reich was transferred to the southwest of France, except one *kampfgruppe*, which remained in Russia (alongside the Leibstandarte) until April 1944.

The division was re-formed as a panzer division, while more than 9,000 new recruits had to be found. Equipment only arrived slowly from Germany, and the deficiencies, especially in vehicles, were great. This would have important consequences, because the division was unable to send all of its components to Normandy, and the last ones only left Toulouse at the end of July.

By June 1, the Das Reich Division only had 617 operational trucks, but it did have 235 working SdKfz 251s. Thanks to various reinforcements, in Normandy it fielded 83 Panzer IVs, 80 Panthers and 45 StuG IIIs, though it would not receive any reinforcements whatsoever after reaching the front.

One of the 42 StuG IIIs, from 2nd Panzer Division Das Reich, in May 1944. (Jean Restayn collection)

In southwest France, a motorized column of 2nd SS Panzer Regiment moves forwards along a narrow path. The Panzer IVs belong to the 5th, 6th, and 7th companies of 2nd Battalion. (Jean Restayn collection)

In Profile:
Panther Medium Tanks

Panther 328, 3rd Company, 1st Battalion, 1st SS Panzer Regiment. The presence of spare track on the turret means that the tank number has had to be painted on the side of the gun shield.

Panther Ausf. A no. 304, 3rd Company, 1st Battalion, 12th SS Panzer Regiment, just before the landings.

As early as June 6, 1944, the 2nd SS Panzer Division Das Reich was put on alert and some wheeled elements began heading to the front. On June 8, several groups were sent on missions to support other German units beset by Resistance fighters. Das Reich itself suffered ambushes, and in one case exacted a horrific revenge on a helpless village called Oradour-sur-Glane.

On June 11, the division was subordinated to Army Group B and assigned to Seventh Army Reserve. By June 13 the division had reached the Domfront sector, and by the 16th, wheeled vehicles and men were grouped near Mortain.

Moving the armored units took longer, as the railyard at Montauban had been smashed by bombers and most of the Loire bridges destroyed. The Panther battalion reached Le Mans on June 19, but for weeks the Das Reich Division was not whole. As well as some units left around Toulouse due to lack of transport, a *kampfgruppe* commanded by Otto Weidinger was allocated to support the 352nd Infantry Division, composed of 2nd Battalion, 2nd SS Panzergrenadier Regiment, three Panzer IV companies, and a battery of StuG IIIs.

By July 1, 1944, only 11,195 of the 17,283 men of the division had arrived in Normandy and numerous tanks were still undergoing maintenance (23 Panzer IVs and 46 Panthers). The division had 50 Panzer IVs, 26 Panthers, and 36 StuG IIIs operational. The functioning Panzer IVs were almost all in the *kampfgruppe* assigned to the 352nd Infantry Division.

Panther Ausf. A no. 213, 2nd Company, 1st Battalion, 9th SS Panzer Regiment, 9th SS Panzer Division Hohenstaufen.

Kommandeur Heinz Harmel, commander of the Frundsberg Division, is saluted by two of his officers, in front of an SdKfz 251 Ausf. D, parked in front of a farm. (Jean Restayn collection)

The division's artillery was not very well equipped, with 22 towed pieces, six Wespes and five Hummels. There were 21 Pak heavy guns. The truck situation was even worse, the journey from southwest France having caused a great many breakdowns and damages. The Das Reich Division had only 768 functioning trucks and 227 half-tracks.

At the end of June the division's Kampfgruppe Weidinger, which had been assigned to support 352nd Infantry, was put under the command of II SS Panzer Corps in order to fend off the British Operation *Epsom*. Fighting alongside 9th SS Panzer Division Hohenstaufen, the KG's losses were significant, with 180 killed, 408 wounded, and 126 missing.

The 9th SS Panzer Division Hohenstaufen

Created in France in 1943, the Hohenstaufen Division left the west in the spring of 1944, as part of II SS Panzer Corps, to be sent urgently to the Russian front. There it helped defeat a Soviet offensive near Tarnopol that threatened to destroy 1st Panzer Army, and suffered about a thousand casualties. It was then put in reserve in eastern Poland before being ordered back to France on June 12.

The division's ranks were not at full strength: out of a supposed total of 19,855 men, they were missing 1,239 officers, NCOs, and men, and almost all the Hiwis—volunteers, short for Hilfswilliger—(retaining only 52 Russian volunteers instead of the 1,055 planned). Amongst the officers the shortfall was greatest: 26 percent of the officers, and 23 percent of the NCOs.

As for resources, the Hohenstaufen suffered from the same problem as the other divisions: it only had two thirds of the vehicles it was intended to field.

Tanks were seriously lacking, because the Panther regiment, which didn't leave for Russia, was still being trained in Mailly-le-Camp. On June 9, 1st Battalion, 9th SS Panzer Regiment did have 79 Panthers (of which 39 were in transit from Germany), but they were not fully operational. They would be sent to Normandy as soon as possible.

As for the artillery, the Hohenstaufen had 28 towed pieces, 12 Wespes and six Hummels; but there were no antitank weapons because the panzerjäger battalion had remained in Russia. An antitank company would be improvised in Normandy in July, with Pak 40 guns found here and there within the division. These were in fact the three antitank pieces original to each panzergrenadier battalion.

The 10th SS Panzer Division Frundsberg

This division has not been as well studied as the 9th SS Panzer Division Hohenstaufen and there are few surviving photographs of it. We do, however, know its composition just before D-Day.

The Frundsberg was originally called Karl der Grosse (Charlemagne), but from October 3, 1943, it was renamed Frundsberg, after a German knight from the late middle ages, renowned as an excellent infantry tactician, but also known for his lack of mercy, notably during the pillaging of Rome in 1527. Quite an inspiration for an SS division.

Along with the Hohenstaufen, the Frundsberg headed to the Russian front in the spring of 1944 to receive its baptism of fire, only to be called back to the west on June 12.

The division was incomplete: 1st Battalion, 10th SS Panzer Regiment never left France but it was not operational and would only join the Frundsberg in 1945. The whole of the armor in this division rested on 2nd Battalion, 10th Panzer Regiment, and there again things were amiss, with only 39 Panzer IVs, 38 StuG IIIs, and three Panzer IIIs. Of all the German armored divisions in Normandy, the Frundsberg had the smallest number of tanks.

War Crimes

Part of the Das Reich Division was ordered to the Tulle-Limoges area on 8 June, where they relieved some army troops in the city of Tulle. The following day, in reprisal for the killing of around 40 German soldiers by the Maquis resistance, they massacred 99 men and deported another 149 to Germany. On 10 June a battalion of the division, commanded by SS-Sturmbannführer Diekmann, massacred 642 French men, women, and children in the village of Oradour-sur-Glane in Limousin. Diekmann alleged the massacre was in retaliation for partisan activity in the area.

German commanders protested the action and began an investigation, but this was halted after Diekmann and many of the men involved were killed in action during the Battle of Normandy. A military tribunal in 1953 found a number of the SS soldiers involved in the massacre guilty of murder.

Max Wünsche, commander of the Hitlerjugend's SS Panzer Regiment, on board a commander's Panther. (© through Jean Restayn)

As for the panzergrenadiers, there were also gaps—three of the 21st SS Panzergrenadier Regiment's battalions were not at full capacity—at only 83 percent, 75 percent and 73 percent of their respective official allocations.

Overall, the 10th SS Artillery Regiment was well equipped, with 11 Wespes (out of an assigned 12), six Hummels, 12 10.5cm guns, 12 15cm Howitzer and four 10cm guns. There was no panzerjäger battalion. Of the 18,000 men due to form the division, 1,984 were missing; worst affected were the panzergrenadiers.

The transfer from Poland began on June 12, and the division regrouped in Normandy from June 24. The division moved to the front on the night of the 25th and 26th. On June 30, 13,552 men were ready to fight. That very day they would advance to resist the British Operation *Epsom*, during which II SS Panzer Corps saved the day for the Germans.

The 12th SS Panzer Division Hitlerjugend

While the Frundsberg has not been the subject of much literature, that is not the case for the Hitlerjugend.

The division was put on the drawing board in June 1943, after Germany's gigantic losses in Russia, with the idea to form a separate division from the Hitlerjugend organization, specifically drawing on those born in the first half of 1926. As boys in the Hitlerjugend they had already been trained in athletics, fieldcraft, and basic shooting, as well as being subject to political indoctrination, so that it was not a leap to convert them to soldiers upon their coming of age.

The officer cadre was drawn from the 1st SS Panzer Division Leibstandarte Adolf Hitler, and included Fritz Witt as division commander, Kurt Meyer and Wilhelm Mohnke as heads of the panzergrenadier regiments, and Max Wünsche as commander of the panzer regiment.

In June 1944, the division was deployed to Normandy, which allowed it to intervene on the front as early as June 7, 1944. It comprised 20,510 men, which made it a very large division, but it had its own weaknesses. First of all, this figure takes into account a replacement battalion, which was not in Normandy but in Arnhem, with 2,438 men. Secondly, it was missing a lot of trained staff: 144 officers and 2,192 NCOs.

As to its tank complement, 98 Panzer IVs were available on D-Day. However there were only about 50 Panthers available on June 1; another account from June 10 mentions 66. Thirteen missing Panthers were sent from Germany on June 7. The rest of the division was well equipped, especially in artillery. The half-tracks were numerous, with 306 SdKfz 251s on June 1.

Wilhelm Beck, liaison officer between the 12th SS Panzer Division and the 1st Panzer Division, two units for which he fought. He was killed on June 10, 1944, by an Allied air raid near Caen. (© through Jean Restayn)

In Profile:
Panzer IV Ausf. H no. 618

Panzer IV Ausf. H no. 618, 6th Company, 2nd Battalion, 12th SS Panzer Regiment, Division Hitlerjugend. Steffi was the name of the tank commander's girlfriend.

Since the SS Hitlerjugend was the first Waffen-SS division to arrive at the invasion front, and fought around Caen throughout the month of June, we will hear more of it in detail in the pages that follow.

The 17th SS Panzergrenadier Division Götz von Berlichingen

The only SS division to fight the entire Normandy campaign in the American sector, the 17th SS Panzergrenadier Division was formed in the regions of Saumur, Poitiers and Châtellerault, France on October 3, 1943. Alerted to the Allied landings on D-Day, it was among the first reinforcements on the ground, and experienced its first full baptism of fire in Carentan against the 101st Airborne Division. From June until the beginning of Operation *Cobra*, it attempted to stop the advance of the U.S. First Army between Carentan and Saint-Lô.

The Götz von Berlichingen (GVB) staff came essentially as transfers from other SS divisions or from instructional staff. The troops were young, 42 percent being only 19 years old, meaning that they suffered from both a lack of training, and combat experience. The division also contained a number of conscripts and foreign volunteers.

On June 1, a third of the men had only received 22 weeks of training, and the rest 25. Furthermore the division was short 233 officers—40 percent of the senior officers were missing—not to mention 1,541 NCOs missing from the official quota, despite there being a surplus of 741 soldiers. On June 1, the numbers were as follows: 584 officers, 3,566 NCOs, 14,204 men and 959 Hiwis. The total was 18,354 men, but the extra men could not compensate for the lack of officers.

As for materiel resources, the deficiencies were huge. In mid-May, the division had only 257 trucks. By June 1, the most obvious shortages in comparison to the table of equipment were: 1,008 instead of 146 machine guns; 8 of 21 7.5cm infantry howitzers; 275 of 410 motorbikes; 1,104 instead of 22 cars; 245 of 1,441 trucks; and 10 of 245 artillery tractors.

In place of tanks, the division possessed 42 Sturmgeschütz IIIs and IVs, which were used within 17th SS Panzer Regiment, and a few Marders within 3rd Battalion, 17th SS Panzerjäger Regiment (three Marders armed with a 7.62cm Russian gun, and nine Marders with 7.5cm guns).

The division was put on alert on the evening of June 6, and prepared to move out to Normandy on June 7. The only unit to head towards the landings zone from June 7 was 17th SS Panzer Reconnaissance Battalion (SS Panzer Aufklärungsabteilung 17). The reconnaissance unit left its encampment very early to mark out the route to Normandy. As the division was already being harassed by Allied bombers, it was decided that only secondary roads should be used. The StuGs and armored vehicles of the division were loaded onto trains in the Mirebeau station. A StuG III was destroyed and three men killed by an air raid when the convoy entered the La Flèche station, to the south of Le

Refueling Tiger no. 009, Stab, from 101st SS Heavy SS Panzer Battalion. (© through Jean Restayn)

Mans. At the end of the day on June 8, 17th SS Panzer Reconnaissance Battalion was less than 20 kilometers from Saint-Lô and on June 10, the first exchange of fire took place between advance elements of the division and American paratroopers, at Graignes.

However, most of the division remained immobile south of Saint-Lô until June 11, due to the lack of trucks. Two panzergrenadier battalions even resorted to bicycles to get to Normandy. Its first major fights, southwest of Carentan, started on June 13.

Götz von Berlichingen

17th SS Panzergrenadier Division Götz von Berlichingen was named after a 15th-century German mercenary knight who, after losing a hand in battle, wore a mechanical iron hand. This hand became the emblem of the division. (Drawing by Emil Eugen Sachsse, 1843–1887)

In Profile:
Organization of SS Divisions in Normandy

1st SS Panzer Division Leibstandarte Adolf Hitler

- 1st SS Panzer Regiment
- 1st SS Panzergrenadier Regiment
- 2nd SS Panzergrenadier Regiment
- 1st SS Panzer Artillery Regiment
- 1st SS Flak Artillery Battalion
- 1st SS Nebelwerfer Battalion
- 1st SS Sturmgeschütz Battalion
- 1st SS Panzer Reconnaissance Battalion
- 1st SS Panzerjäger Battalion
- 1st SS Panzer Engineer Battalion
- 1st SS Panzer Signals Battalion
- 1st SS Divisional Supply Troops
- 1st SS Field Replacement Battalion

2nd SS Panzer Division Das Reich

- 2nd SS Panzer Regiment
- 3rd SS Panzergrenadier Regiment "Deutschland"
- 4th SS Panzergrenadier Regiment "Der Führer"
- 2nd SS Panzer Artillery Regiment
- SS Panzerjäger Battalion
- 2nd SS Flak Battalion
- 2nd SS Nebelwerfer Battalion
- 2nd SS Motorcycle Battalion
- 2nd SS Panzer Reconnaissance Battalion
- 2nd SS Engineer Battalion
- 2nd SS Signals Battalion
- SS Field Replacement Battalion

9th SS Panzer Division Hohenstaufen

- 19th SS Panzergrenadier Regiment
- 20th SS Panzergrenadier Regiment
- 9th SS Panzer Regiment
- 9th SS Panzer Artillery Regiment
- 9th SS Panzer Reconnaissance Battalion
- 9th SS Panzerjäger Battalion
- 9th SS Flak Battalion
- 9th SS Panzer Engineer Battalion
- 9th SS Panzer Signals Battalion
- 9th SS Sturmgeschütz Battalion
- 9th SS Observation Battery
- 9th SS Divisional Supply Troops
- 9th SS Medical Company

10th SS Panzer Division Frundsberg

- 10th SS Panzer Regiment
- 21st SS Panzergrenadier Regiment
- 22nd SS Panzergrenadier Regiment
- 10th SS Motorcycle Regiment
- 10th SS Panzer Artillery Regiment
- 10th SS Flak Artillery Battalion
- 10th SS Panzerjäger Battalion
- 10th SS Panzer Engineer Battalion
- 10th SS Panzer Signals Battalion
- 10th SS Replacement Battalion

12th SS Panzer Division Hitlerjugend

- 25th SS Panzergrenadier Regiment
- 26th SS Panzergrenadier Regiment
- 12th SS Panzer Regiment
- 12th SS Panzer Artillery Regiment
- SS Motorcycle Regiment
- 12th SS Flak Artillery Battalion
- 12th SS Nebelwerfer Battalion
- 12th SS Panzer Reconnaissance Battalion
- 12th SS Panzerjäger Battalion
- 12th SS Panzer Engineer Battalion
- 12th SS Panzer Signals Battalion
- 12th SS Supply Battalion
- 12th SS Maintenance Battalion
- 12th SS Divisional Supply Troops
- 12th SS Provisioning Battalion
- 12th SS Medical Battalion
- 12th SS War Correspondent Platoon (Motorized)
- 12th SS Military Police Troup
- 12th SS Field Post Office (Motorized)

17th SS Panzergrenadier Division Götz von Berlichingen

- 37th SS Panzergrenadier Regiment
- 38th SS Panzergrenadier Regiment
- 17th SS Panzer Reconnaissance Battalion
- 17th SS Sturmegschütz Battalion
- 17th SS Panzerjäger Battalion
- 17th SS Engineer Battalion
- 17th SS Artillery Regiment
- 17th SS Flak Battalion

First Battles of the Hitlerjugend

As soon as it arrived near Caen, Sepp Dietrich's I Panzer Corps headquarters was charged with launching a counteroffensive in the direction of the sea, but confusion reigned on the front line and the attack's progress would face many problems. There was also hesitation in OKW, which remained unsure if the Normandy landings were the real invasion or just a feint. Given the wide dispersal of Waffen-SS divisions—from Belgium to the Paris area to southern France—decisive action was necessary if the Allies were to be prevented from establishing a deep bridgehead.

Two Panthers from 12th SS Panzer Regiment. (© through Jean Restayn)

Troops of an SS Panzergrenadier Regiment march along the main street of Le Sap in early 1944. From left to right, the officers on the forefront are SS-Hauptsturmführer Bolgk, Hauptmann Bäderkele and SS-Untersturmführer Fuss. (P. Tiquet collection)

Von Schweppenburg's Criticism

It is useful to remember the conditions on the ground early on June 6, 1944. Army Group B commander Erwin Rommel was away in Germany. Geyr von Schweppenburg was not there either, and many general officers had been called away to a wargame conference at Rennes. So from June 7, 04:00, it was Dietrich's I SS Panzer Corps which assumed the commanding role for the three armored divisions nearest to the beachheads—21st Panzer Division, the Panzer Lehr Division, and the 12th SS Panzer Division Hitlerjugend. Panzer Group West was to be activated as a headquarters commanding the strategic reserve immediately upon confirmation of the invasion, but positive authority was slow in arriving from Berlin. Meantime the Germans under direct fire, as so often in the war, had to improvise.

Following the campaign, von Schweppenburg wrote this rather odd comment:

> The first action that I SS Panzer Corps took should have been to ignore contradictory orders, in as much as no one within the senior staff had the slightest idea on how to best use armored vehicles, apart from perhaps Rommel and his chief of staff [Speidel]. Even then Rommel's knowledge was only based on his experience in Africa, and Normandy is not Africa. Moreover, due to the Allies' air superiority, Rommel had lost all faith in the possibility of a mobile armored war.

Panzer Group West was formed in January 1944 in France. Geyr von Schweppenburg and Gerd von Rundstedt agreed that in the event of an Allied invasion it should be held in reserve behind the front, ready to crush any Allied breakthroughs. Rommel disagreed, maintaining that unless an invasion was counterattacked immediately, Allied airpower would prohibit any concentration. The result was that Hitler insisted that the reserve could only be committed with his permission. Thus on June 6, Panzer Group West did not move. By June 8, Geyr had rushed three panzer divisions north to defend Caen. The panzer group suffered heavy losses during the Battle of Normandy, and the surviving elements would be redesignated Fifth Panzer Army in August.

This statement can be explained by the difference of opinion between Rommel and von Schweppenburg on the use of the panzer divisions, the former wanting them near to the coast, to intervene on D-Day itself, the latter being in favor of the creation of a large mobile force inland, capable of launching a massive counteroffensive wherever required. In the end the panzers' placement was a rough compromise.

Von Schweppenburg was right on one thing: Rommel had never used his armored divisions in North Africa in a traditional way, rather he had always dispersed his units, in contrast to the doctrine used to brilliant effect in France in 1940, which required that the panzer divisions be massed to create a breakthrough on the front line, and should never be dispersed.

In a Normandy village, grenadiers from 12th SS Panzer Division Hitlerjugend move up the line. (P. Tiquet collection)

SS-Untersturmführer Uphoff's section, taken during training in Belgium before the landings. (P. Tiquet collection)

Rommel could get away with cavalry-type skirmish tactics in the desert, facing a less agile and not very creative opponent. Also the numbers in the desert had very little in common with those in Normandy. Nevertheless, to assume that Rommel lacked the instincts for how to deal with a formidable opponent, in whatever form, is misguided. Certainly the Waffen-SS officers who made up much of his command had seen enough large-scale warfare in Russia.

On June 6, 21st Panzer Division launched—without much conviction—the only attack led by tanks, without Rommel. Though it found a gap open toward the coast, it did not achieve any concrete results, and it is therefore fair to say that for the Germans, June 7 was the most important date: the Allied bridgehead was still precarious.

Another criticism that stands out in Geyr von Schweppenburg's report is the way in which the counteroffensive was planned: its objective was to advance on Courseulles-sur-Mer (the site of Juno Beach), in coordination with an advance from the Panzer Lehr in the west and from the 12th SS Panzer Division in the east, covered by 21st Panzer Division.

Geyr would have preferred a coordinated attack by all three divisions, which would give it more weight. Besides, the direction of the attack was meant to allow Panzer Lehr to take Bayeux back, but by doing so it had to divert its march towards the west, which widened the offensive front and so the Panzer Lehr and Hitlerjugend lost contact with the 21st Panzer Division. The reasons for this dissociation are not obvious in Geyr's report, but perhaps I SS Panzer Corps' commanding officers had limited faith in the 21st Panzer Division, or in its ability to disengage from the defensive line it already held.

Rommel inspecting troops of 21st Panzer Division, France, May–June 1944. (Bundesarchiv, Bild 101I-300-1865-08)

In Profile: Field Marshal Erwin Rommel

Undoubtedly the most famous of German World War II commanders, Erwin Rommel encountered his greatest task as commander of Army Group B in June 1944. There he not only had to guard hundreds of miles of French coastline, unsure where the Allies were going to attack, but had to wrestle with his own high command over where to allocate his panzer reserves.

Born in 1891, Rommel established a dashing reputation as a small-unit commander in the Great War, and afterward wrote a book, *Infantry Attacks*, that is still studied in military colleges today. In 1940 France he commanded the 7th Panzer Division, which spearheaded the German drive to the Channel, forcing the British evacuation and French capitulation. The next year he faced the British again in North Africa, and in a dizzying series of maneuvers with his AfrikaKorps backed them up nearly to the Nile, until finally being overwhelmed by numbers at El Alamein.

Promoted to field marshal, he commanded briefly in northern Italy and was then assigned to northern France as the inevitable Anglo-American invasion drew near. He personally believed the assault would come at Calais, but Normandy was also a possibility, and Hitler himself (for reasons still unknown) intuited that it would be the target. With his indefatigable energy, Rommel built up the Normandy defenses in the weeks before the invasion, creating obstacles to both amphibious and airborne forces. His desire to keep the panzer reserve close to the beaches, however, was denied.

When the invasion came, Allied airpower inhibited a concentration of panzers, just as Rommel had predicted, so that he was forced to fight an improvised battle. Nevertheless, the Germans were still holding their own when he was severely wounded, on July 17, by an Allied fighter-bomber.

On July 20, German Army officers attempted to kill Hitler, and some of the conspirators mentioned Rommel's name as Hitler's possible successor in Berlin. Though not part of the plot, Rommel had been implicated, and while convalescing from his wound that October he was visited by Hitler's representatives and offered the option of suicide rather than a trial. His death was announced as ensuing from his combat wound, and he was given a state funeral. Hitler also declared a national day of mourning.

Training with a Schwimmwagen from the Hitlerjugend, shortly before the landings. (P. Tiquet collection)

What is certain, however, is that the planned concentration for a counteroffensive took much longer than expected, and it could not be launched on June 7—which is hardly surprising given that the Panzer Lehr and the Hitlerjugend had barely arrived in Normandy—but neither were they ready by the 8th, or even the 9th.

I SS Panzer Corps' Version

We know I Panzer Corps' version of events thanks to a report by SS-Brigadeführer Fritz Krämer, corps chief of staff.

First, it insists on the fact that confusion reigned throughout Normandy when I SS Panzer Corps established positions. Many of the phone lines had been cut, and the corps did not want to use the radio, so as to avoid its presence being tracked by the Allies. It was therefore liaison officers who had to make contact with various units in the field, which was made all the more difficult for the 716th Infantry Division—which was still fighting on the coast—because no one knew the exact locations of the British.

Finally, secret codes were distributed in the afternoon of June 7, and transmitted to 21st Panzer Division. There was, however, no contact with the Panzer Lehr. The corps was eventually informed that it was supposed to cross the Thury-Harcourt bridge, to the south of Caen, and a courier was dispatched there to give the codes to the Panzer Lehr. Unluckily the officer was killed in the early morning of June 7 by a truck whose driver did not see him.

The codes were not given to the armored division, which only established contact with I Panzer Corps that evening, after more than 12 hours' delay.

Exercising his authority was not easy for Krämer and his staff, especially as wild rumors abounded: Caen had been flanked, the Americans had moved south of Bayeux, the British armored vanguard was near Falaise, etc.

Moreover, the roads were jammed with stragglers from the coastal divisions: not just individual soldiers, but also rear-echelon troops, men from the Todt organization, and Hiwis—individuals that Krämer branded "cowardly riffraff." To avoid full-scale panic, Krämer ordered that security posts be set up along the roads leading to Falaise and towards the south of Caen to arrest or re-organize these crowds.

To get a better idea of the situation on the ground, Krämer visited the command post of 716th Infantry Division. What he saw there did not please him: the best elements of the division were still fighting on the coast, but they were isolated in their bunkers and the rest of the division was quite unable to relieve them.

The other unit largely engaged against the British to the north of Caen was the 21st Panzer Division, but it was holding a precarious position across the river Orne and its canal, with its reconnaissance and antitank battalions to the east of the river, combating British paratroopers, and the rest to the west. It could not therefore be used whole.

Hauptmann Bäderkele, still wearing his Heer uniform, checking the barrel of a machine gun. (P. Tiquet collection)

This recruit from the Hitlerjugend Division seems particularly young. He has put two grenades in his belt. (P. Tiquet collection)

The Schimmwagen going deeper in the water. To compensate for the lack of phone communication, dispatch runners were often used to send orders. (P. Tiquet collection)

Kurt Meyer, early 1943. (Bundesarchiv, Bild 101III-Ludwig-006-19)

In Profile:
Kurt Meyer

Kurt Meyer was born in 1910 to a family of modest means, though his father had been a master-sergeant in the Great War. After working as a policeman, in 1930 Meyer joined the Nazi Party and then the Leibstandarte Adolf Hitler, though he was a trifle short of the unit's specifications. By 1937 he had risen to the rank of captain, and when World War II began, he lost no time proving himself an elite soldier, winning the Iron Cross 2nd Class in Poland, the 1st Class in France, and then the Knight's Cross in Greece. By then he was commanding the Leibstandarte's Reconnaissance Battalion and won the Oak Leaves in Russia in 1943. After the war he was dogged by testimony that his unit's actions often involved atrocities.

In summer 1943 Meyer was transferred to the fledgling SS Hitlerjugend Division to command its 25th SS Panzergrenadier Regiment. As one of the first reinforcements to arrive on the invasion front, Meyer's unit was once again accused of atrocity, this time the murder of Canadian prisoners. (Through the rest of the campaign the Canadians responded in kind.) With the death of SS Hitlerjugend commander Fritz Witt to naval gunfire on June 14, Meyer took command of the division, becoming Germany's youngest general at 34. When the Germans finally collapsed in Normandy, Meyer barely made it out of the Falaise Pocket, but became separated from his command and was ignominiously captured by Belgian partisans.

As a prisoner in Britain he expressed astonishment at news of the Germans' Ardennes Offensive, partly led by the SS Hitlerjugend Division, as he assumed his old command had been destroyed. After the war he was sentenced to death for killing Canadian prisoners in Normandy, but the sentence was later commuted and he was freed from prison in 1954. Meyer remained active in SS veterans associations until he died in 1961.

Von Rundstedt during a visit to the Hitlerjugend Reconnaissance Battalion. (P. Tiquet collection)

In the evening of June 7, General Fritz Bayerlein, commander of the Panzer Lehr, finally arrived before Krämer; he announced that the Thury-Harcourt bridge had been damaged by air raids and had to be strengthened before the tanks could use it. This would delay the division.

As for the Hitlerjugend, the panzergrenadier units were getting ready as planned at their assembly points, but the tanks were lagging behind. It was becoming obvious that an immediate attack by the full 12th SS Panzer would be impossible. Nevertheless, on the night of June 6, Kurt Meyer, commander of the HJ's 25th Panzergrenadier Regiment, arrived at the command post of the 716th (Coastal) Division, where he also met with Lt. General Feuchtinger, commander of 21st Panzer. Upon being informed that a joint attack by 12th SS and 21st Panzer was planned for the morning, Meyer studied the map and then, as Feuchtinger related, "turned to me with a confident air and said, 'Little fish! We'll throw them back into the sea in the morning.'"

Meanwhile, I SS Panzer Corps had still not been able to make contact with its neighboring corps (to the west) and thus did not know precisely where the front was. The only thing known for certain, thanks to intercepted radio messages, was that the Americans were holding a bridgehead north of Bayeux (Omaha Beach), and the British another one north of Caen.

It was only on the evening of the 7th that the Luftwaffe was able to undertake a reconnaissance mission, which confirmed a breach of 8–10 kilometers between the 1st SS Panzer Corps and the Army Corps.

These two volunteers from the 12th SS Panzer Division are wearing trousers made of Italian camouflage fabric. (P. Tiquet collection)

Action was urgently needed, but the Panzer Lehr would not be ready on the 8th. Sepp Dietrich, who had meantime conferred with 12th SS commander Fritz Witt late on the June 6, decided to launch two units that were more or less operational into an interim attack along the road north of Caen, to Lion-sur-Mer—21st Panzer Division on the right and 12th SS Panzer Division on the left. The main focus of the attack was on the left, with maximum artillery support in this sector. The Panzer Lehr would intervene as soon as possible to the west of the Hitlerjugend. In Krämer's report it was stressed that this plan was not optimal, but the situation called for an emergency measure.

The Progress of the Counterattack

The I SS Panzer Corps counterattack was one of the only ones undertaken by the Germans in the Caen sector. It took place piecemeal on June 7th and 8th, launched by elements of the Hitlerjugend as they arrived in the sector. On the latter day it was joined by a *kampfgruppe* from the Panzer Lehr, the rest of the division not yet having completed preparations. The 21st Panzer Division was under heavy British pressure and could only commit meager elements, which did not manage to make much headway.

The 12th SS Panzer Division Hitlerjugend therefore advanced pretty much alone towards the Canadians, until it was brought up short by a British naval bombardment, the ferocity of which even Russian front veterans had never seen. The Hitlerjugend did manage

A young SS-Unterscharführer examines the burnt wreck of a Sherman tank, pierced by an antitank shell or by the hollow charge of a Panzerfaust. (P. Tiquet collection)

Close-up shot of a Hitlerjugend StuG III. In the background is an antitank Pak 40 gun and two heavy SdKfz 7. (P. Tiquet collection)

to establish a solid front on a line between the Orne and Blainville and a position situated 5 kilometers north of Caen. The Germans would remain there for several weeks. This position had the great advantage of blocking the British and preventing them from reaching Caen and the open ground to its south. However, the attack cost the Hitlerjugend dearly. In fighting against the Canadians during the first week, they suffered well over 1,000 killed and wounded.

The end of the counteroffensive, which had only truly been led by one division, showed the Germans' inability during the first days of the Battle of Normandy to retake the initiative. They were only able to react. Dietrich, who received an order from Seventh Army to resume the offensive on June 9 in order to re-capture Bayeux, was not able to comply: his divisions were in contact with the enemy (Panzer Lehr now in full grapple with British XXX Corps) and unable to lead another counteroffensive unless relieved by the infantry. However there were no infantry divisions available.

This cover from *Die Woche* magazine, August 16, 1944, shows a young Hitlerjugend Division soldier with a MG 42. (P. Tiquet collection)

Grenadier Otto Funk, about whom so much was written thanks to this famous photograph, carrying ammunitions and spare MG 42 barrels for his colleague K. Schuh. Funk survived the war. (P. Tiquet collection)

Sepp Dietrich in 1944. (Bundesarchiv, Bild 183-J27366)

In Profile: Sepp Dietrich

Sepp Dietrich stood considerably apart from the average German general in World War II, and as such his merits have been a subject of controversy. Far from being an aristocrat, or general staff-trained, he rose to the rank of sergeant in the Great War (though winning the Iron Cross 1st Class) and afterward became a policeman before finding his true calling in the late 1920s: head of Adolf Hitler's personal bodyguard—the Leibstandarte. In that role he was instrumental in the "Night of the Long Knives," when the SS decapitated its political rival within the Nazi Party, the SA, to secure Hitler's power.

By the time World War II began, the Leibstandarte had been converted into a combat regiment, with Dietrich in command, and repeated successes in Poland, France, Greece, and Russia led to its growth into a full SS panzer division. A hands-on battlefield leader, Dietrich kept near the front, inspiring his men during crises and encouraging them in success. Though some say he was unable to comprehend a military map, he was beloved by his hard-fighting troops. In 1943 he was made head of a new I SS Panzer Corps, to consist of the SS Hitlerjugend and Leibstandarte divisions. However, in Normandy his corps originally consisted of the SS Hitlerjugend, 21st Panzer, and Panzer Lehr. This was the corps that withstood the original Allied onslaught on Caen.

Dietrich (or "Obersepp" as his men called him) finally encountered the Peter Principle in late 1944, when he commanded Sixth SS Panzer Army in the Ardennes Offensive, an elevated post too complex for his skills. It was at this point that von Rundstedt made his enduring judgment of Dietrich, "Decent, but stupid." Nevertheless, as a pure battlefield commander, Dietrich had proved exceptional. He had the additional value of being one of the few ranking generals able to speak to Hitler frankly—the former corporal always willing to listen to the former World War I sergeant. After serving a sentence for war crimes, Dietrich died in Bavaria in 1966, at age 74. Six thousand people attended his funeral.

This young grenadier has just joined the Hitlerjugend. He wears the sniper and proficiency badges. These were supposed to be forbidden, but the wearing of them was tolerated. (P. Tiquet collection)

Following its initial advance, I SS Panzer Corps went on the defensive. It was not able to undertake any further large offensives, only one-off counterattacks.

The Battle in Detail

We have seen the main threads of this day of counteroffensives, so let's now look at it in more detail. It is important to remember that the SS Hitlerjugend Division, in contrast to the 21st Panzer Division, far from being present on the front on June 6, had to come from about 200 kilometers away, and engage in the battle without any time for preparation.

When the landings began on the morning of June 6, the 12th SS Panzer Division was put on alert in the Dreux region west of Paris. The I SS Panzer Corps had anticipated a joint action of three panzer divisions against the Allied bridgehead as early as D-Day itself: the 21st Panzer Division, stationed near the coast, the 12th SS Panzer Division, and finally the Panzer Lehr Division.

In practice, this plan proved completely impossible to carry out: only the 21st Panzer Division was able to counterattack, and even then, quite late on June 6.

Hitlerjugend grenadiers run with caution across a farm courtyard in Normandy. (P. Tiquet collection)

The 12th SS Panzer Division Hitlerjugend left Dreux that day, with orders to concentrate first in the sector of Lisieux before moving to Caen—a detour which extended the journey by a good 40 kilometers. The division's commander, Gruppenführer Fritz Witt, gave an order for an attack at midday on June 7. It would consist only of "attacking the enemy who has landed, jointly with the 21st Panzer Division, and to throw it back to the sea." Evidently, this operation would have been easier to achieve on the 6th, but the division was at least 20 kilometers too far south to intervene at that point.

During the night of June 6/7, in order to prepare for the attack, Witt met Feuchtinger, commander of 21st Panzer Division, and Oberst von Oppeln, who commanded 22nd Panzer Regiment of the division. But the two divisions still needed to get into position.

Jochen Dedow, Werner Ehrsam and Theo Stahl, 12th SS Panzer Division, on the turret of their Panther. (Jean Restayn collection)

A section looking for its position on the map. Note the variety of uniforms, a mix of Italian and German camouflage fabric. (P. Tiquet collection)

25th SS Panzergrenadier Regiment Prepares

One of the first units to get ready in the early hours of June 7, 1944, was Kurt Meyer's 25th SS Panzergrenadier Regiment, supported by about 50 Panzer IVs from the 2nd Battalion of the 12th SS Panzer Regiment. Meyer set himself up in the Ardenne Abbey, on Caen's northwest edge. Taking advantage of a good vantage point on the abbey's top floor, Meyer could see all the way to the coast. (A number of authors have written that Meyer climbed the abbey's bell tower to make his observations, but the abbey did not have a steeple in 1944.)

What Kurt (nicknamed "Panzer") Meyer saw prompted him to make some quick decisions: there was a column of Shermans obliquely approaching both the abbey and the concealed lines of his panzergrenadier regiment. He could not know that the Allies' plan had called for Caen to be captured by the evening of June 6, but he understood straightaway that if his position was overwhelmed, nothing could stop the Allies from taking the city.

Luckily for the Hitlerjugend, the Allies—Canadians—were not aware of the German troops' presence in this sector and carried on advancing none the wiser toward Caen and its outlying Carpiquet aerodrome. Meyer warned his men to be ready and also liaised with Max Wünsche, commanding officer of the 12th SS Panzer Regiment.

First Fight, First Success

There is an argument that Meyer should have stayed in position, ready to engage his men in the joint offensive planned for 16:00 hours. But the Germans had devised their plan without

Waffen-SS from the Hitlerjugend observe with satisfaction the side of a Sherman riddled with holes. (Jean Restayn collection)

Several officers of 12th Panzer Division Hitlerjugend studying a map: SS-Sturmbannführer Erich Urbanitz, Karl-Heinz Prinz, and Karl Bartling. (Jean Restayn collection)

considering that the Allies would also be attacking, and now an entire Canadian column was passing unawares, broadside in close range of the 25th SS Panzergrenadiers. Meyer waited for the enemy formation to fully stretch out on the Caen-Bayeux road in front of his hidden positions, and then gave the order to fire. Suddenly the whole German line revealed itself with a wall of flame—mainly antitank pieces and the guns of the Panzer IVs, but the panzergrenadiers joined in with their machine guns. One by one, unable to fight back with effect, the tanks of the 27th Armoured Regiment, 2nd Canadian Armoured Brigade, were immobilized: 28 Shermans were destroyed on that June 7. The accompanying infantry, North Nova Scotia Highlanders of the Canadian 9th Brigade, were brushed aside by the panzergrenadiers' fire. As the panzers surged, Canadian infantrymen made a stand in the village of Authie, holding out for almost an hour before being overrun.

A number of the Canadian soldiers captured by the Hitlerjugend during the fighting, including soldiers of the North Nova Scotia Highlanders, were executed at the Ardenne Abbey, the regimental headquarters of 25th Panzergrenadier Regiment. The killings were the core of the charges at Kurt Meyer's war crimes trial in December 1945. As he was commander of the regiment at the time, he was found responsible for the murders, and guilty of inciting his troops to commit murder.

Panzer IV no. 618 from 2nd Battalion, 12th SS Panzer Regiment, probably photographed when the division was still in Belgium. (© through Jean Restayn)

Sherman T14112, destroyed by the Hitlerjugend Division. This is the same machine seen on page 63. (© through Jean Restayn)

Fritz Witt, commander of the Hitlerjugend, was killed on June 14, by Allied naval artillery.
(Jean Restayn collection)

Already the End of Maneuver Warfare

The Allied reaction was very quick—it was not the air force that intervened, but the powerful Canadian artillery, joined by British guns, and supported by rapid-firing warships off shore. The panzergrenadiers were forced to take cover and could not advance any further. Worse still, their right flank was exposed because the tanks of the 21st Panzer Division had not advanced, waiting for the official start-time of the attack. The Canadians took advantage of this and attempted to advance. They pushed back the 1st Battalion, SS Panzergrenadier Regiment, and threatened the German position, but SS Pak guns soon stopped them, and the Canadians were forced back again.

Pursuit was impossible, because as soon as the Germans tried to advance, they were set upon by the 12th and 13th Field Artillery Regiments, the 3rd Anti-Tank Regiment, and the machine guns and mortars of the Cameron Highlanders of Ottawa.

SS Gruppenführer Witt wanted to throw the 26th SS Panzergrenadier Regiment into the battle. But it had barely arrived, and had had no time to establish a position when it was attacked by the 7th Canadian Infantry Brigade. Mohnke's 26th SS could offer little resistance as the Canadians approached within actual sight of Carpiquet airfield. But aware of the setback of 9th Brigade on their left, the 7th Brigade cautiously halted its advance to secure the ground already gained. By the end of the day, Kurt Meyer had likewise called off his attack, his decision aided by the fact that his flanks were not secure. Although in the Audrieu and Cristot sector, the 12th SS Reconnaissance Battalion had come to stand by Meyer's men, contact had not yet been established with the Panzer Lehr Division, which was only beginning to arrive in the area. If the 50th (Northumbrian) Division had attacked at this juncture, it would have met very little resistance.

The official Canadian history recorded the engagement with the Hitlerjugend soldiers: "The powerful German attack made us lose our balance and inflicted heavy losses on us. The Germans however, were unable to exploit their success and the danger to our bridgehead was avoided."

Taking Back the Initiative

After June 7, both the Germans and Canadians thought that they might be able to gain the upper hand the next day. Rommel, who had always thought the battle could only be won in the first few hours, worried about the inability of his troops to counterattack in mass. He ordered a counteroffensive for June 8, to be launched by the three Panzer divisions on the ground: the 21st Panzer Division, the 12th SS Panzer Division Hitlerjugend, and Panzer Lehr.

In practice, this proved impossible. The advance liaison officers from Panzer Lehr stated that their division could not arrive in strength until the 9th, at best, or more likely on June 10. 21st Panzer Division had meantime suffered heavily during the two previous days, and only had 55 available tanks; furthermore it was unable to disengage from its main opponent, the 3rd British Infantry Division, while it also had to straddle the Orne River to contain the 6th Airborne's bridgehead. Panzer Meyer's 25th SS Panzergrenadier Regiment could do no better: it had engaged its three battalions on June 7 and had no reserve. It was not in a position to help clear the front around Buron, without which Caen would be taken.

This only left—in the Caen sector—26th SS Panzer Regiment. Alone, it could not even attempt to push all the way to the sea. But at the very least it could open a way towards Bayeux for the tanks of the Hitlerjugend, by taking three villages held by the 7th Canadian Infantry Brigade: Norrey-en-Bessin, Putot, and Bretteville-l'Orgueilleuse. The assault was due to start on the morning of the 8th.

June 8, 1944, 03:30

At 03:30, under the cover of darkness, three companies of 1st Battalion, 26th Panzergrenadier Regiment, left their positions near Cheux. The Germans hoped to surround the Regina Rifles Regiment, which was holding Norrey, by launching a pincer attack, with the 1st and 3rd Companies advancing to the right of Norrey, and 2nd Company on the left. The assault was led by Sturmbannführer Bernhard Krause, who chose to forsake the element of surprise by employing SdKfz 251s.

As the Panzergrenadiers crossed the Mue, they came up against brisk resistance from the Canadians, who laid down suppressing fire, supported by their artillery. The Germans were forced to stop in their tracks. One of the company commanders was killed by machine-gun fire. The two companies soon had to dig themselves in.

On the right, the 2nd Company made better progress, and even passed Norrey to set itself up by the railroad. It could not however, attack Norrey alone, and so fell back across the railroad to the hamlet of Cardonville, near Bretteville.

It is hard to understand how and why the Germans launched such an operation—without seeking to surprise the enemy and without artillery support. According to Hubert Meyer, in his book on the 12th Panzer Division Hitlerjugend, this was due to Canadian radio interferences, which scrambled communications between German artillery observers and their pieces. In any case, the aborted attack in the morning cost the Germans about 25 casualties. Canadian losses were minimal.

Badly Coordinated Attacks, But Efficient Nonetheless

The young recruits of the 12th SS Panzer Division Hitlerjugend had no prior battle experience, though most of its staff had come from battle-hardened SS divisions, including the Leibstandarte. What became clear from the start was that the HJ's teenaged rank-and-file were eager to fight, and to launch attacks without hesitation—or even proper coordination.

This Canadian Sherman Firefly was destroyed by the Hitlerjugend. (Jean Restayn collection)

In Profile:
German Armor

A SdKfz 250, 102nd SS Heavy Panzer Battalion. Note the pink unit insignia.

A StuG IV, 17th Panzergrenadier Division Götz von Berlichingen. The use of the insignia is not certified.

Front and back views of a SdKfz 250, 12th SS Panzer Division. The profile of this machine, armed with an anti-air piece Breda can be found on page 26.

A still taken from a movie showing a column of the Hitlerjugend Division, with a Kübelwagen, motorbikes, a SdKfz 251 and a Panther, all going through a village in Normandy. (Jean Restayn collection)

So was this why the attacks of the 8th were so poorly coordinated? The three battalions of 26th Panzergrenadier Regiment all attacked on that day, but not together.

That said, even a poorly timed attack can achieve results, and this was the case for the 2nd Battalion, led by Sturmbannführer Siebken. At 06:30, Siebken's companies departed Le Mesnil-Patry, and quickly covered the kilometer and a half that separated them from their target, Putot. This time, Canadian radio interference was not effective, and the assault was supported by artillery and mortar fire. However, they could not break through the defenses at Putot: A Company, the Royal Winnipeg Rifles, resisted desperately, and were responsible for heavy losses among the young German recruits, who were forced to abandon the assault—at least temporarily.

Before resuming the attack, Siebken requested artillery reinforcement, and so shells of all kinds, including from 88mm guns, devastated the village and caused severe casualties among the Canadians. Moreover, German snipers in the upper levels of houses in the village—some may have been remnants of the 716th Infantry Division—started to apply pressure to the Canadian defenders.

At 09:30 Siebken's men went back into the fray. By midday they had crossed the railway and completely surrounded Putot, trapping three Canadian companies inside. With their ammunition running low, the Canadians tried to break through to rejoin their intact D Company outside the village, but very few managed to get through. The others were killed, wounded or pushed back inside the village, where they ended up surrendering. Putot was thus taken by the 2nd Battalion, 26th SS Panzergrenadier Regiment. The Royal Winnipeg Regiment was all but destroyed.

No One Is Ready to Give Up

At first, the 3rd Canadian Infantry Division thought that it would be able to retake the village with artillery alone, but this did not prove possible; even when Putot, already badly damaged, was crushed under the fire of four artillery regiments. Observers however, realized that the Waffen-SS were not falling back.

Brigadier Harry Foster, commander of 7th Canadian Infantry Brigade, then resolved to launch a ground attack to take back the village. For this purpose he created a battlegroup made up of the brigade's reserve battalion, the Canadian Scottish Regiment, reinforced with two squadrons from the 6th Armoured Regiment and elements of the Cameron Highlanders of Ottowa, equipped with machine guns and mortars. The 12th and 13th Field Regiments provided artillery support.

The battle group assembled in the woods near the Bergerie Farm and prepared to attack with two companies ahead, two in reserve, and tanks covering their flanks. The attack started around 20:30, behind a creeping barrage of incredible intensity. In the first instance the Hitlerjugend put up strong resistance and killed two Canadian officers leading the troops. However, the intervention of the Shermans proved a decisive factor as the Waffen-SS had been unable to get their Pak guns to Putot because of the Canadian artillery. Before it was too late, the Hitlerjugend managed to fall back to the railroad and the Canadians made their way into the ruins of Putot by 21:30. The battle raged on during a large part of the evening.

The Canadians regained the ground, which was an indisputable victory, but the cost was especially high: the Canadian Scottish lost 125 men and the Winnipeg Rifles had lost

Panther no. 308, 3rd Company, 1st Battalion, 12th SS Panzer Regiment, was captured by the British, who took this picture. (© Tank Museum, Bovington)

A fine view of Kretschmar's Panzer IV no. 536. (Jean Restayn collection)

First prisoners in the hands of the Canadians. (© through Jean Restayn)

A 17-year-old in the signals service. (P. Tiquet collection)

In Profile:
Panther Medium Tanks

A Panther with no turret number from 1st SS Panzer Division Leibstandarte Adolf Hitler.

View from the back and profile of Panther no. 219, 12th Panzer Regiment, Hitlerjugend Division.

A SdKfz 234 of Ustuf Uphoff company, before the fighting began. (P. Tiquet collection)

256. On the German side, the losses were significantly lower: 19 killed, 58 wounded, and 21 missing.

And so concluded the second day of 12th SS Panzer Division Hitlerjugend's engagement. The respite would be short-lived because from June 11, the 2nd Canadian Armoured Brigade would launch a new attack to break the German front line between Le Mesnil-Patry and Cheux, south of Norrey-en-Bessin, directly into the center of the SS Hitlerjugend's sector.

Panthers' Defeat

After the end of the fight in Putot on June 9, Hitlerjugend went on the defensive. The first battles on the 7th and 8th had been costly, the division needed reorganizing, and a renewed attack with the Panthers on June 9 had promptly failed, with heavy losses and no result. In the space of a few minutes in the early afternoon, SS Panzer Regiment 12's 3rd Company lost seven of its 12 Panthers, and the others fell back immediately, so as not to compound their losses. The only consolation had been to make the enemy more wary of the Hitlerjugend's willingness to counterattack. As early as June 8, Bernard Montgomery had informed London:

A truck of the 12th SS Panzer Division Hitlerjugend, on June 6 or 7, 1944. The streets are deserted and the sky is overcast. (© ECPAD)

"The Germans are doing everything they can to hold on to Caen." The Allied commander would begin planning moves to outflank the city, even while maintaining pressure head-on.

The Mue Valley

The Mue is not a large river, but its name is remembered because of the battle fought there on June 11, 1944. The Allies' plan was a simple one: push the Germans past the Mue, in order to close the breach between the 7th and 9th Canadian Infantry Brigades. Essentially this meant taking the small village of Rots.

With this objective in mind, the Allies put their resources together: 46 Royal Marine Commando was to lead the attack, supported by tanks of the Fort Garry Horse. The North Shore Regiment and the French-Canadian Régiment de la Chaudière would follow behind. Initially the Commandos' attack went well and the three villages were taken almost without a fight.

Things changed when the 46 RM Commando approached Rots, strongly held by the Waffen-SS. A ferocious battle began with the two opponents engaged in bloody street fighting. The Commandos called in the Fort Garry Horse's Shermans, but these were engaged by the Hitlerjugend's Panthers and three tanks were quickly put out of action in the village square. A bit later, three other Shermans were destroyed. However, little by little, the Commandos made progress and during the night, the Hitlerjugend fell back. Their decision to do so is partially explained by the fact that fighting also raged in the southwest, in the direction of Cheux. The village of Rots was too isolated to the north to be held, and the Germans wanted to shorten their line.

The losses from both sides were heavy: the regimental diary of the 12th SS Panzer Division indicates 22 killed, 30 wounded and 15 missing. The 46 RM's diary gives a total of 22 killed and over 80 wounded. There is however a contradiction between the Hitlerjugend's numbers and those of the Régiment de la Chaudière, which counted the dead Germans around Rots on the morning of the 12th and found 122. The discrepancy could exist because the French Canadians may not have distinguished which units the dead Germans belonged to, and another German division had fought in this sector: the 716th Infantry Division—or rather what was left of it. The coastal division had taken the brunt of the fight on June 6, and naturally fell back to the south to hold the front with the Hitlerjugend. The dead in question could have belonged to this undersung division.

An Attack Moved Forward by 24 hours

While the commandos were clearing up the Mue Valley, the British 69th Infantry Brigade was attacking further to the west, in the direction of Bronay and Fontenay-le-Pesnel. At the last minute, the British commanders realized the potential difficulties of an isolated attack and the Canadians received an order to join it. In itself this was a good idea, as the Canadian offensive provided a link between 69th Brigade and 46 RM Commando, creating a consolidated offensive front line. However, at the last minute the assault was moved forward from June 12th to the 11th. At 04:00, during a conference with the Armoured Brigade's

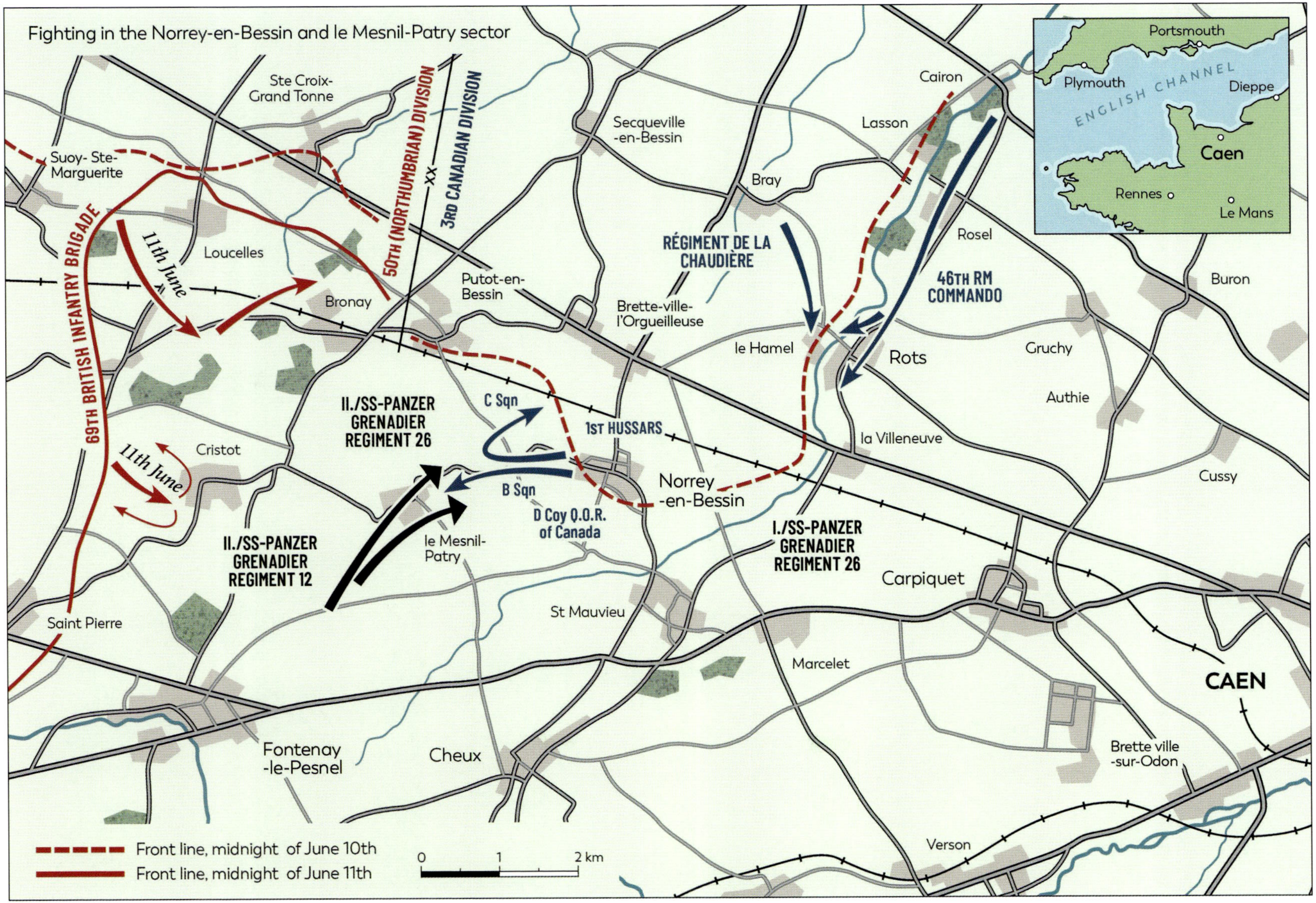
Fighting in the Norrey-en-Bessin and le Mesnil-Patry sector
Ste Croix-Grand Tonne
50TH (NORTHUMBRIAN) DIVISION
XX
3RD CANADIAN DIVISION
Secqueville-en-Bessin
Cairon
Lasson
Portsmouth
Plymouth
ENGLISH CHANNEL
Dieppe
Caen
Rennes
Le Mans
Suoy-Ste-Marguerite
69TH BRITISH INFANTRY BRIGADE
11th June
Loucelles
Bronay
Putot-en-Bessin
Bray
RÉGIMENT DE LA CHAUDIÈRE
Brette-ville-l'Orgueilleuse
le Hamel
Rosel
46TH RM COMMANDO
Rots
Buron
Gruchy
Authie
II./SS-PANZER GRENADIER REGIMENT 26
C Sqn
1ST HUSSARS
la Villeneuve
Cussy
Cristot
11th June
B Sqn
Norrey-en-Bessin
D Coy Q.O.R. of Canada
II./SS-PANZER GRENADIER REGIMENT 12
le Mesnil-Patry
I./SS-PANZER GRENADIER REGIMENT 26
Carpiquet
Saint Pierre
St Mauvieu
Marcelet
CAEN
Fontenay-le-Pesnel
Cheux
Brette ville-sur-Odon
Verson
Front line, midnight of June 10th
Front line, midnight of June 11th
0
1
2 km

In Profile:
Panther Medium Tanks

A Panther Ausf. A, 10th SS Panzer Regiment, Frundsberg Division. The turret number painted onto the spare track is quite original.

A profile view and detail of Tank Commander Barkmann's Panther Ausf. A, 4th Company, 1st Battalion, 2nd SS Panzer Regiment, Das Reich Division.

A young SS-Unterscharführer from the Hitlerjugend Division, wearing several insignia— including the Wound badge—which indicate that he is a veteran of the fighting on the Russian front. He probably previously served with 1st SS Panzer Division Leibstandarte Adolf Hitler, who supplied some of the division's officers. (P. Tiquet collection)

staff, the 1st Hussars' Commanding Officer was informed that his men would lead an attack within 24 hours, i.e. June 12. But at 08:00 a counter-order arrived that the attack would take place that same day, with the regiment launching its drive at 13:00.

The commanding officer of the supporting infantry battalion, the Queen's Own Rifles, met Brigadier R.A. Wyman of the 2nd Canadian Infantry Brigade and Lieutenant-Colonel R.J. Colwell, of the 1st Canadian Hussars (also known as the 6th Armoured Regiment), in order to prepare the attack. Nobody knew why it had been moved forward, and a rumor quickly spread that the Germans were falling back and that the Shermans were going to give them chase. In the morning the infantrymen of the Queen's Own Rifles arrived and the officers of both units tried to design a combined operation, despite the lack of information on the opponent.

Confusion also reigned among the Germans because Panzer Group West's command post had been destroyed by Allied air attack the day before, with heavy officer losses—although Geyr von Schweppenburg had escaped with his life. Additionally, an attack planned for dusk on June 10, led by the 21st Panzer Division and the 12th SS Panzer Division Hitlerjugend, had to be abandoned because there was not enough reserve strength to hold a defensive front if the panzer divisions left their lines. This then, forced them to await the arrival of reinforcing infantry divisions. There was also a growing breach in the German line south of Bayeux. The inability of the Germans to promptly build a coherent front prevented them from launching a powerful counteroffensive. The 12th SS Panzer Division, which had suffered losses since June 7, was on the defensive on the 11th when the British and the Canadians attacked.

The Canadians' battle plan was rushed due to the lack of time between the order and the launch of the attack, and because the British did not warn them of the procedure for coordinating with their neighboring units, especially 46 RM Commando to their left and the 69th Infantry Brigade to their right. No artillery preparation was planned, and the troops genuinely thought that the offensive would be a walk in the park. They just needed to take Le Mesnil-Patry, and then march on to Cheux.

A Bad Start

The 1st Hussars left their positions in Bretteville by late morning in the following order: B Squadron, C Squadron, RHQ Squadron, A Squadron. The infantry climbed aboard the tanks. The start line was south of Norrey-en-Bessin, which involved going through the village, since bypassing it was impossible because of minefields put in place by infantry after they conquered the village. Certainly the village offered shelter and hid the tanks' movements, but the streets were narrow. The route through the village required a sharp turn past a large-steepled church, meaning that the Shermans had to maneuver carefully to get around it.

B Squadron was involved in making these turns when the men of the 12th SS Panzer Division positioned outside Norrey noticed the characteristic dust cloud of a tank unit on the move. The officers ordered artillery and mortar support and it wasn't long before shells began to fall on the village. The 1st Hussars' commanding officer tried to find a different route, but his tank hit a mine and he was forced to go back to the church sector on foot to try and speed up the move.

Contemporary postcard, showing a poster encouraging the Hitler Youth (Hitlerjugend) to join the division of the same name. "Auch Du" means "You too." (P. Tiquet collection)

B Squadron finally reached its start line at 14:20, long past the agreed time of 13:00, and began its advance. While crossing a cornfield and scanning the ground for mines, a tank commander suddenly realized that the field concealed waiting panzergrenadiers. Infantrymen scattered off the tanks as a wild gunfight ensued among the rows of corn. The panzergrenadiers opened fire with machine guns and mortars, stripping the tanks of their infantry support.

Otto Funk, wearing his machine-gun ammunition belt, on the front cover of the June 21, 1944 issue of *Stuttgarter Illustrierte*. (P. Tiquet collection)

A Chaotic Battle

B Squadron had no other choice than to keep charging forward, while spraying the ground ahead with machine-gun fire. C Squadron followed to the right with A Squadron to the left, while the infantry battle raged behind them.

When B Squadron came to a rise on the edge of Le Mesnil-Patry it encountered a line of antitank guns on the reverse slope. As several tanks entered the village, Captain

In Profile:
Panzer IV Medium Tanks

Insignia of 2nd SS Panze Division Das Reich.

Panzer IV Ausf. H no. 622, 6th Company, 2nd Battalion, 2nd SS Panzer Regiment 2, Das Reich Division, with its yellow insignia.

Profile and back view of Panzer IV Ausf. J no. 715, 7th Company, 2nd Battalion, 1st SS Panzer Regiment, Leibstandarte Adolf Hitler Division.

7 15

622

Panther no. 313, partially camouflaged, in a dominating but exposed position, meaning it is at risk even if its fire range is excellent. (© through Jean Restayn)

Wildgoose, leading No. 4 Troop, broke radio silence to announce that he could also see tanks straight ahead. At the same moment, Squadron commander Major Marks warned that they were receiving antitank fire from the right. But whose guns were they? Lt. Colonel Colwell assessed that the fire was coming from the British 50th Division on the right, accidentally shooting at the 1st Hussars. Consequently he ordered his squadrons to cease fire and show their identification pennants. He then tried to get in touch with B Squadron, but to no avail. Major Marks tried something simpler: he got out of his tank to check that the C Squadron tanks had put their pennants out. He realized then that far from dying down, the fire had increased, and that one by one the Shermans were being taken out. He warned Colwell and told his tanks to break contact with the enemy. C Squadron, hammered between friendly and enemy fire, pulled back, as did A Squadron. At the tip of the spear, however, B Squadron was taking the brunt of a full counterattack by the 12th SS Panzer Division Hitlerjugend.

Back in Norrey the situation was becoming worse by the minute, due to incoming artillery and mortar fire. The Regina Rifles, holding the village, suffered heavy losses as the advanced Canadian tanks and infantry fell back. While the depleted C Squadron did its best to cover the withdrawal, the task became more difficult as the panzers emerged from cover and numerous Shermans were hit and set alight.

Fiasco in Norrey

Major Marks withdrew as soon as all his remaining tanks fell back towards Norrey. The village was a picture of destruction. The large church steeple had been hit by artillery and its rubble blocked the streets, so much so that the tanks could not get through and were stranded as the Germans approached. To avoid disaster, the leading tanks were ordered to break down a wall and find a new way out of the village. One of the tanks broke down a wall and found itself in a garden, from which it easily found a way. Another tank broke down a different wall, but this one was the wall of a house and the Sherman fell through the floor into the basement.

The panzers were getting closer. Sergeant Boyle of A Squadron managed to hit a Panther, a small success against the disaster engulfing B Squadron. All of its forward tanks had been destroyed—the only survivors being two that had broken down before reaching the fight. The 19 others were just smoking wrecks, victims of the Hitlerjugend's panzers and antitank guns. C Squadron had also seen great losses, only seven of its 21 tanks making it back.

This could have had disastrous consequences if the 12th SS Panzer Division had continued on with its attack. To avoid a breach in the front line, 1st Troop of A Squadron along with C Squadron's seven surviving tanks took up a relatively sheltered position on the railroad, to try and form a roadblock before Bretteville.

The infantry had also suffered greatly: D Company of the Queen's Own Regiment of Canada lost 96 men that day. In total, out of the 179 casualties suffered by the Canadian infantrymen in the attack of Le Mesnil-Patry, 114 had been killed, an unusually high proportion.

Looking for Survivors

> The battle at Le Mesnil-Patry is remembered as "The Black Day" within the 1st Hussars and the Queen's Own Rifles. The casualties from this one battle accounted for around one third of the 1st Hussars' dead for all of World War II.

When the 1st Hussars withdrew from the line in order to regroup, it was missing more than 100 men. B Squadron alone had lost 61 killed (and missing who were never found even after the war). The eyewitness accounts of the few survivors enable us to better understand the engagement. After the first success that was the entrance into Le Mesnil-Patry, the Shermans had to face camouflaged antitank weapons and well-hidden panzers, who held their fire right up until the moment the Allied tanks were upon them. After this, everything happened very fast. Within a few minutes, all the tanks had been hit, some were on fire, others simply immobilized. Some crews escaped, but promptly realized that the place was full of Waffen-SS, with snipers targeting the officers. There was no hope of help from the infantry because the Queen's Own Rifles were also in trouble.

The Canadians claimed 14 destroyed enemy tanks, which would balance a little the loss of the 1st Hussars' 34 Shermans. However, the Hitlerjugend had in total lost only three Panzer IVs. The loss in men, especially in panzergrenadiers during the wild fight in the cornfield, was much heavier, with 196 killed, wounded and missing, though these losses pale in contrast to those of the Canadians.

A SdKfz 251 Ausf. D, 12th SS Panzer Division. The divisional insignia is clearly visible. (© through Jean Restayn)

A Few Surprising Questions

To account for their failure, the Canadians implied that their attack was launched at the same time as a massive offensive from the 12th SS Panzer Division, citing the artillery concentration in Le Mesnil-Patry and Norrey-en-Bessin as proof. Survivors recounted that they suddenly found themselves in the middle of infantrymen launching an assault. They also speak of a number of tanks much too concentrated to be part of a mere defensive line. This argument was even been put forward on June 12 by General Simonds, Commanding Officer of the 2nd Canadian Corps, for whom the "futile [attack] of Mesnil-Patry stopped the attack of a Panzer Division, thus preventing the 7th Canadian Infantry Brigade from being cut in half, and at the same time helping the 7th Armoured Division's advance on the right flank."

When compared with the German movements however, these arguments do not hold up, because the German records explicitly show that the offensive planned for June 10 had been postponed and was eventually canceled while they waited the arrival of further divisions. The 12th SS Panzer Division Hitlerjugend had therefore not received an order to attack.

It was rumored that the Germans found—in a destroyed halftrack the day before the battle of Le Mesnil-Patry—the communication codes of the Royal Navy. They used it to direct battleships' and cruisers' fire against Canadian troops. Nothing in the Canadian and British reports neither confirmed—nor denied—this rumor.

What is certain however, is that the battle of Le Mesnil-Patry ended the possibility of any kind of offensive by the 3rd Canadian Infantry Division for the rest of June. This unit had fought from the landings on June 6 and on the five following days. After the battle of Le Mesnil-Patry, and following the heavy losses in Putot, the 3rd Canadian Infantry had to refit and regroup, only taking part in offensives again in July. By contrast, the German division they faced from June 7, the SS Hitlerjugend, had to stay in the line and fight continuously until the end of August 1944, resting only for a few days at a time, and always in close proximity to the front. This however takes nothing away from the bravery of the Canadian troops engaged at Le Mesnil-Patry on June 11, 1944.

The Desert Rats and a Tiger

The 12th SS Panzer Division Hitlerjugend did not remain the only Waffen-SS unit in Normandy for long. From the south, the 17th SS Panzergrenadier Division Götz von Berlichingen was completing its difficult 200-mile trek to reach Carentan, a key city that stood between the two American beachheads of Omaha and Utah. From Versailles, despite damaging air attacks, the 101st SS Heavy Panzer Battalion was moving into the I SS Panzer Corps sector south of Caen. However, this did not mean that it was possible to launch a German counteroffensive, especially as on June 10, the command post of Panzer Group West was destroyed by an air raid, with most of the senior officers killed and the communication equipment annihilated. This momentarily paralyzed the German panzer units in Normandy.

Hauptscharführer Berhausen's Tiger no. 323. As with all tanks from 3rd Company, the I SS Panzer Corps insignia is highly visible on its front armor. (© Bundesarchiv)

The confusion among the commanding officers was great. So much so that on June 11, Friedrich von der Heydte's 6th Fallschirmjäger Regiment, which had been waging a desperate fight against the U.S. 101st Airborne Division, received an order to abandon the town of Carentan. At least, that is what von der Heydte wrote after the war. The withdrawal was undertaken on the afternoon of 12th, with most of the regiment leaving the town, even as General Ostendorff, the commander of the 17th SS Division, presented himself to von der Heydte to tell him he had orders to reinforce the paratroopers to ensure Carentan's defense.

There is other evidence in the matter. In fact, the war diary of Seventh Army is categorical: the Army warned the paratroopers as early as June 10, at 13:00, and then again on June 11, at 11:45, of the SS division's impending arrival. According to General Pemsel, Seventh Army's Chief of Staff, von der Heydte's decision was simply due to the stress of battle, and the fact that his gallant fallschirmjäger were almost out of ammunition. Whatever the exact cause of the withdrawal, the consequence was clear: the Götz von Berlichingen would have to retake Carentan, as opposed to defending it, or using it as a base for an offensive. Its initial attack against a battalion of the 101st Airborne nearly broke back into the town,

One of the 14 half-tracks destroyed by Wittmann between Villers-Bocage and Hill 213. The SdKfz 251/1 belongs to the reconnaissance platoon, 4th Company, 101st SS Heavy Panzer Battalion. (© Bundesarchiv)

Tiger no. 311 on the Amiens plain. Raassch and von Westernhagen, the battalion commander, are standing behind the turret. (© Bundesarchiv)

except that elements of the U.S. 2nd Armored Division arrived from the beaches just in time. The 17th SS Panzergrenadiers would grapple with ever-increasing American strength through the rest of the campaign.

A Tough Beginning for 101st SS Heavy Panzer Battalion

On June 12, while the Götz von Berlichingen was encountering its unpleasant surprise at Carentan, the 101st SS Heavy Panzer Battalion—consisting of Tiger tanks—was arriving at its staging area between Caen and Falaise. Like other German units, its approach march had been disrupted by destroyed rails and bridges, and near Versailles it had suffered a devastating air attack. According to Fritz Krämer, chief-of-staff of I SS Panzer Corps, the battalion lost half its strength. In truth the attack had cost 27 men, nine of them dead, which is not nearly half a battalion. However, in destroyed or damaged tanks the loss was considerable. By the time it got to Normandy, the 101st SS Battalion had only 15 operational tanks from an authorized complement of 45. Others were undergoing short-term repair, but in the meantime the battalion's 1st Company had nine tanks ready for action, the 2nd Company five, and the 3rd Company only one.

Tiger no. 331 in training before D-Day. (© Bundesarchiv)

The Sherman Firefly Allakeefek, abandoned intact by the British, would yield interesting information to the Germans, who hadn't previously known of this type of Sherman armed with a 17-pdr. (© Bundesarchiv)

Despite its losses, the 101st SS Heavy Panzer Battalion soon more than proved its value. To better understand the turn of events, we must take a look at the situation on the front line of the I SS Panzer Corps, where British-Canadian pressure was steadily growing.

A Massive Breach

The SS Panzer Corps' front line was in jeopardy on its left wing. Indeed, the Panzer Lehr Division, now grappling with the British XXX Corps, had been unable to establish proper communications with its neighboring LXXXIV Corps, which was fighting the American V Corps to the west. Only a few recon units could be spared to patrol the wide gap, while the Germans fervently hoped for the arrival of 2nd Panzer Division to solidify their front.

On June 12, British forces seized the village of Tilly-sur-Seulles, and were immediately counterattacked by Panzer Lehr. The village would change hands numerous times until its formerly picturesque streets were reduced to utter rubble. Farther to the west American troops had plunged southward to seize the key town of Caumont, on high ground well inland from the coast. German LXXXIV Corps, including the remnants of the 352nd

A Tiger I, captured by the Sherwood Rangers on June 26, 1944, during the fight around Rauray. It has withstood many impacts that didn't manage to pierce the armor, except probably the one on the driver's vision block. In the background we can see a burnt Panther from the 12th SS Panzer Division. (© IWM B6047)

SS-Obersturmführer Wittmann in his black tank uniform, with his crew, who have adopted the Waffen-SS camouflage panzer uniform. (© Bundesarchiv)

Tiger no. 334 destroyed on the road from Rauray to Tilly-sur-Seulles. (© through Jean Restayn)

Tiger no. 231 is being towed by no. 232, after the fights of Villers-Bocage. This was actually forbidden by the manual for obvious reasons: the Tiger was heavy and fragile and its engine was not designed to move 56 tons times two. (©Bundesarchiv)

Tanks of 101st SS Heavy Panzer Battalion climb the hilly road from Gournay-en-Bray to Les Andelys, north of the Seine. (© through Jean Restayn)

A Sherman Firefly, 1st Northamptonshire Yeomanry, 33rd Brigade in the Odon sector. The Fireflies were the British answer to the Tigers: the heavier gun could impact on the German heavy tank, contrary to smaller calibers. However, the Firefly's armor was weak and could not withstand the Tiger's shots. Combat between the two types of tank then became all about speed. (© Tank Museum)

Division which had fought so well at Omaha, had been forced to concentrate against the incursion, losing its link to the defenders of Caen. On that day the commander of LXXXIV Corps, Erich Marcks, was killed by a fighter-bomber as he desperately tried to organize a counterattack. Partly informed by the Americans, and in part by their own recon, the British realized that a gaping hole had opened in the German front. While part of XXX Corps would keep Panzer Lehr tied down in front, the British 7th Armoured Division—the famous "Desert Rats" from North Africa—could swing to the west around Tilly, cut through the American zone, and plunge into the open ground south of Caen, centered on the town of Villers-Bocage. The I SS Panzer Corps would be practically cut off.

On the afternoon of June 12 the 7th Armoured Division drove into the breach between the 352nd Infantry and the Panzer Lehr. This truly seemed like a walk in the park for the leading 22nd Armoured Brigade, which was followed by 131st Brigade. Up to this point every kilometer they had taken had been ferociously defended, but now there seemed to be no German resistance. A single antitank position caused some delay until dusk, when 7th Armoured chose to bivouac for the night, just six kilometers short of Villers-Bocage.

Early on June 13 the British column advanced again, led by A Squadron, 4th County of London Yeomanry, equipped with Cromwell tanks and a few Sherman Fireflies, followed by infantrymen from the 1st Rifle Brigade and command vehicles. Behind these flowed the

SS-Obersturmführer Wittmann, hero of Villers-Bocage. This photograph was taken in Normandy, and his Knight's Cross with Oak Leaves is clearly visible around his neck. (© through Jean Restayn)

In Profile: Michael Wittmann

Michael Wittmann has been celebrated as the most successful panzer ace of World War II, though some historians have argued that his success was more attributable to the superiority of the Tiger tank, and questioned his strategic and tactical performance in battle.

He joined the army in 1934, then the SS two years later, applying for the 1st SS Panzer Division Leibstandarte Adolf Hitler, where he was trained as a driver. Initially he commanded an armored car in a reconnaissance unit, and then after the Poland campaign he was moved to command a Sturmgeschütz III. His skill became apparent during the campaign in the Balkans, and he was awarded the Iron Cross Second and then First Class for taking out enemy tanks. Following further training, he was finally paired with the feted Tiger tank, returning to the front line just in time to fight in the Battle of Kursk. On the first day, Wittmann destroyed 12 T-34s, and by the end of the battle he had taken out 30 tanks and 28 antitank guns. In January 1944, Wittmann was awarded the Knight's Cross for destroying 88 tanks and tank destroyers. In April, the Tiger company of Leibstandarte Adolf Hitler was transferred to the 101st SS Heavy Panzer Battalion, based in Beauvais, France, and Wittmann became commander of 2nd Company. Wittmann is probably best known for his victory at Villers Boccage, which made him a household name in Germany. He was killed in battle on August 8, when his Tiger was ambushed by Canadian Shermans.

rest of these two battalions, along with the 8th King's Royal Irish Hussars, the 1/7th Queen's Royal Regiment, and the 26th Anti-Tank Battalion.

Meeting no opposition, the British column passed through Villers-Bocage and down the road beyond, toward the key height of Hill 213, which provided a vista of the entire countryside south of Caen. For reasons that still remain unclear, 7th Armoured did not take proper recon precautions on its right flank, which seems rather lax on a front where fierce resistance had previously been the norm. Indeed, the long British column was being observed, if only by a solitary German panzer.

One Tiger against an Armored Brigade

What happened on the morning of June 13 is well known; however, it remains an unprecedented exploit in the history of armored warfare, and a reinforcement of Napoleon's dictum a century earlier: "In war men are nothing; a man is everything." In this case the man would be Michael Wittmann, Germany's greatest tank ace on the Eastern Front, who was now about to play a similar role in the battle for Normandy.

As we have seen, the 101st Heavy Panzer Battalion had only arrived the evening before, and it much wanted a day of rest to maintain and repair its Tigers. However, in the emergency it was the only force available to contest 7th Armoured's advance. When Obersturmführer

A famous shot of Tiger no. 131, in the village of Morgny, Eure, not far from Les Andelys. (© through Jean Restayn)

SS-Unterscharführer Bobby Woll, Wittmann's gunner. This shot is taken just after he was decorated with the Knight's Cross. (©through Jean Restayn)

Wittmann, commander of the 2nd Company, was warned of the British move, he decided to intervene straight away. He commandeered SS Unterscharführer Sowa's Tiger no. 222 and advanced toward Villers-Bocage, while the other four operational tanks of his company followed at a distance toward Hill 213.

In a concealed position overlooking the road, Wittman watched the lead British column pouring out of Villers-Bocage. His gunner commented, "They're acting as if they've won the war already," to which Wittman replied, "We're going to prove them wrong." True, he was unaware of the extent of the enemy formation, but attacking alone he knew he had to be drastically outnumbered. Nevertheless Wittmann, like all good officers, knew that the speed of response in a crisis can often turn the tables.

Breaking cover, Wittman's Tiger fired its 88mm gun and destroyed the nearest British tank, a Cromwell. Seconds later it put a Sherman Firefly up in flames. All traffic on the narrow road came to a halt as Wittmann's heavy tank, as if on parade, moved down the column, main gun and machine guns blazing, destroying, one after the other, 14 half-tracks, three Stuarts, two Sherman OP tanks, three more Cromwells, and a dozen Bren Carriers. British return-fire from the flaming road either missed the Tiger or bounced off its thick armor.

Now entering Villers-Bocage itself, Wittmann found himself face to face with B Squadron, 4th County of London Yeomanry. He destroyed another Cromwell and some headquarters vehicles, and brought a building down on top of another tank hiding behind a corner. But now he was under fire himself from antitank guns as well as infantry, sometimes

Churchills from the 31st Tank Brigade, who fought in particular during Operation *Epsom*. Despite its thick armor, the Churchill V and VI were unable to withstand the Tigers' fire. (© IWM B7584)

SS-Unterscharführer Warmbrunn's Tiger, put out of action during the fights in Rauray. (© IWM B6155)

Tiger no. 232 towing no. 231. The tank commander wears the motorcycle coat. (© BA Bild 101I-738-0267-18, Grimm)

Tiger no. 221 on the road to Gournay-en-Bray, with 1st SS Panzer Corps' insignia visible. (© through Jean Restayn)

The burnt carcass of Tiger no. 12 (with 1st Company's insignia visible) was abandoned in Villers-Bocage. It was set alight by a Sherman Firefly from the 4th CLY. (© BA Bild 101I-494-3376-13A, Zwirner)

A nice shot of Tiger no. 101, with a Schwimmwagen waiting for it. (© through Jean Restayn)

in upper stories firing downwards with Piats and grenades. It was no environment for a lone Tiger, and when he lost a track to a 6-pdr gun he and his crew abandoned ship. They were able to escape to the command post of Panzer Lehr, which was already putting together a force of rear-area infantry to march to the sound of gunfire. Panzer Lehr also dispatched a company of 15 Panzer IVs toward Villers-Bocage, while Wittman himself was given a recon vehicle to return to his unit.

The Battle Rages On in Villers-Bocage

On Hill 213, which had been reached by A Squadron of the 4th CLY prior to Wittman's attack, the British picture was no better. When radio operators in Villers-Bocage contacted the battalion's commander, Lt. Col. Lord Cranley to report the dire situation, Cranley replied that atop the hill he was surrounded by Tigers. These were the other tanks of Wittman's company, joined by some Panzer Lehr Mark IVs that had made it out of a nearby workshop. This was Cranley's last communication before he and most of his men surrendered.

Tiger no. 112 in the ruins of Villers-Bocage after being immobilized by a Firefly. (© Bundesarchiv)

Close up of the Sherman Allakeefek. Men from 101st SS Heavy Panzer Battalion are examining the engine. (© Bundesarchiv)

The battle then switched to the village, where the fight became more even, as 7th Armoured's 22nd Brigade went on the defensive, and several Tigers and Mark IVs fell victim to 6-pdr or close-quarters infantry fire. By now the 1st Company of 101st SS Heavy Panzer was also in the fight, though a Firefly destroyed Tiger no. 112, while another Firefly incapacitated Tiger no. 121. In return, the 1st Company put another five Cromwells out of action east of the town, then another eight in the village's streets.

Panzer Lehr infantry had also begun chewing its way through the village, and given the arrival of German reinforcements, 7th Armoured's commander, Gen. Robert Erskine, decided the place was untenable. As the day waned 22nd Brigade pulled out, in coordination with an artillery barrage that turned the vacated streets to rubble. As the fighting ended, 101st SS Heavy Panzer Battalion tallied its impressive total for the day: around 30 tanks destroyed—Cromwells, Shermans, and Stuarts—plus 14 half-tracks, 16 carriers, and 230 prisoners. This success cost the 101st SS Panzers ten men—three of whom were tank commanders—three destroyed Tigers, and a further three badly damaged. Panzer Lehr had also lost a few tanks, plus infantry in the street fighting.

The Germans Hold their Ground

The next day the 7th Armoured's 22nd Brigade laagered in a position for all-round defense, supported by the 131st Brigade, which had somehow failed to participate in the battle of June 13. But no great attack occurred. The British did not seem to realize that 7th Armoured's great right hook had been defeated only by the fortuitous presence of Michael Wittmann and his battalion, supported by improvised scratch forces from Panzer Lehr. Nevertheless, on that day a British patrol captured an advance staff car of 2nd Panzer Division. This renowned division had by no means arrived in force, but it gave 7th Armoured the face-saving excuse that its withdrawal was due to the sudden, unexpected presence of 2nd Panzer.

On June 14 the 7th Armoured Division was pulled back to its start-line, in conjunction with a large airstrike that flattened Villers-Bocage, together with a gigantic artillery barrage

Oscha Ernst's Tiger no. 112 destroyed in the streets of Villers-Bocage, next to a Panzer IV from the Panzer Lehr Division. The difference in size is obvious, especially between the tracks. (© BA Bild 101I-494-3376-7A, Zwirner)

from both XXX Corps and American V Corps guns. Calling upon the participation of V Corps at the end soon came to be seen as another mistake, as it gave the Americans reason, in the post-war literature, to claim that they had "saved" the British from a rout. In point of fact, the Germans had planned no further attacks that day anyway.

Quite apart from the losses inflicted, the British were in shock. Their advance into the breach on the left of the Panzer Lehr had been shattered, and wouldn't restart until the entire ratio of forces in Normandy had shifted. Moreover, the 7th Armoured Division, considered by many to be Montgomery's best foot forward, had taken a fatal blow to its morale. It would not fully recover its reputation for the duration of the campaign, though its long record prior to Normandy remains unblemished.

As for the Germans, the success of Villers-Bocage was a stroke of luck: the propaganda units seized on it and several teams of photographers and cameramen were sent to immortalize the British disaster. Wittmann, who already held the Knight's Cross with Oak Leaves, was recommended for and awarded the Swords, presented personally by Hitler on June 29 at Berchtesgaden.

German Command Attrition in Normandy

A striking aspect of the Normandy campaign was how several German generals fell to Allied fire, causing constant confusion and hesitations in tactical response to the Allied invasion. As early as D-Day itself, Wilhelm Falley, commanding the 91st Infantry (Luftlande) Division, was ambushed and killed by American paratroopers while rushing to the front. Four days after the invasion, the newly established headquarters of Panzer Group West was obliterated by an Allied air strike, after intelligence intercepts revealed its location. Geyr von Schweppenburg escaped with a wound, but most of his staff was killed.

On June 12, Erich Marcks, commanding LXXXIV Corps, which was adjacent to I SS Panzer Corps, was killed by a fighter-bomber as he tried to organize a counterattack to retake Caumont. Two days later, the commander of SS Hitlerjugend, Fritz Witt, was killed by naval gunfire at his headquarters near Caen. At the end of the month Friedrich Dollmann, commanding German Seventh Army, committed suicide after Cherbourg fell, forcing Paul Hausser to vacate his command of II SS Panzer Corps to take over Seventh Army. Of course, Erwin Rommel himself was knocked out of the battle by a Jabo (in that case a Spitfire) on July 17. Later, on July 28, the new commander of 2nd SS Panzer Division, Christian Tyschen, was ambushed and killed on the road by American troops in the Cotentin.

The long reach of Allied firepower, plus the German propensity to lead from the front, created more command losses than expected in the campaign. Ironically, the highest-ranking American commander to die in the war, Lieutenant General Lesley McNair, was also lost in Normandy, as he was accidentally caught on June 25 in a short-bombing by the USAAF.

The Harsh Battle of Normandy

After its brilliant strike on June 13, the 101st SS Heavy Panzer Battalion was forced to feel the grueling effects of the Battle of Normandy, which became more a war of attrition than anything else, with Allied airpower playing a key role.

On June 14, the battalion was reinforced by the late arrival of its 3rd Company. But on the very first night, it was struck by a violent air raid. Two Tigers took a full blast and were set on fire and their crews killed. Another, which was trying to escape the danger zone, fell off a cliff, resulting in its destruction and the death of its crew. Finally the turret of the company commander's tank was ripped off. Four of the Tigers were thus lost before even getting the chance to fight. There were 29 dead and wounded.

On June 15, the 1st Company avenged its losses with another attack on the 7th Armoured Division, destroying five tanks and several antitank guns, for the loss of only one Tiger. The next day Tiger no. 111 was put out of action and its commander, SS-Obersturmführer Hannes Philipsen, killed, which was a severe loss as he was one of the battalion's aces. As the fight continued through June the Germans were losing about one Tiger for every five or six British tanks destroyed. However the German losses were not being replaced, while the Allies' were. The lack of replacement tanks for the Waffen-SS would weigh heavily on the battle.

The 101st Heavy Panzer Battalion was put in reserve around June 25, but on the 26th, another storm broke loose upon the Germans: this time an attack by a full, newly arrived British corps.

Another Tiger from 1st Company, abandoned on June 13 in Villers-Bocage. Its crew had to scuttle it, which explains the turret's unusual position. (© BA Bild 101I-494-3376-5A, Zwirner)

Operation *Epsom*

By mid-June, notwithstanding the ferocity of frontline combat, the greater contest had become which side could build up their forces the fastest—and this was a race the Allies were winning.

Part of the reason was that their intelligence deception campaign, Operation *Fortitude*, had succeeded beyond anyone's imagination. Incredibly, a week after the largest amphibious invasion in history, the Germans still did not recognize the Allies' main effort. The 17 infantry divisions of their Fifteenth Army remained immobile in the north, awaiting another assault at the Pas de Calais. Further, it was only on June 12 that the SS-Leibstandarte Adolf Hitler (in Belgium) and the II SS Panzer Corps (in Poland) were finally given orders to move to Normandy. Even then, their approach march was bloodied by constant Allied air attacks, and delayed by countless ruined railyards and bridges. Meantime the English Channel had become blanketed with 2,000 Allied ships conveying a constant stream of reinforcements to the front. Among the most powerful of these was British VIII Corps, which would next take the lead against the still-threadbare German crust.

Having failed to seize Caen by direct assault from the beaches, and then by thrusting 7th Armoured into a gap in the enemy front, Montgomery now decided to employ brute force. His cudgel would be the VIII Corps, consisting of the 15th (Scottish), 43rd (Wessex), and 11th Armoured Divisions, together some 60,000 men with 700 tanks, supported by as much artillery and airpower as the British could bring to bear. Led by Lieutenant General Richard O'Connor, of North Africa fame, VIII Corps would attack just to the west of Caen, its initial opposition consisting only of the battered lefthand units of the SS Hitlerjugend Division. Montgomery ordered the operation to begin on June 23.

The Weather Saves the Germans

If the timing of Operation *Epsom* had come off as planned, precious little could have prevented a rupture of the German front in Normandy, with the open ground beyond Caen providing an easy Allied stomping ground toward the Seine and Paris. But on June 19 the wind picked up menacingly in the Channel, and soon turned into a gale, and suddenly the entire Allied invasion fleet had to look to its own safety. For three days, until the 22nd, Allied supply practically came to a standstill, as hundreds of small craft floundered on shore, creating more wreckage than on D-Day. The same relentless storm kept the Allied air forces grounded, which was a godsend for approaching SS-Panzer reinforcements. As it turned out, the postponement of *Epsom* by three days comprised the whole sliver of chance upon which the German defense depended.

The Offensive Begins

According to the new British timetable, as a preliminary move on June 25, General Bucknall's XXX Corps was to seize high ground on 12th SS Panzer's far left in order to protect the plunge of VIII Corps into its left-center. But even there the Hitlerjugend responded with its usual obstinacy, and by the end of the day tenaciously clung to the village of Rauray, with isolated riflemen still holding out in Fontenay. XXX Corps did not achieve its mission; nevertheless, Panzer Meyer became so alarmed at this threat to his flank that he ordered the 12th SS's Panther battalion to move from its reserve position to counterattack. This was despite the pleas of his 26th SS Panzergrenadier Regiment, standing alone before VIII Corps, and who through wireless intercepts and recon intelligence knew that an avalanche was about to fall upon it the next morning.

On June 26, hundreds of British artillery pieces, supported by naval guns, plastered the front of the 26th Panzergrenadiers. Then into the carnage and smoke O'Connor's VIII Corps, led by the 15th Scottish Division, began to advance. They first seized the village of Cheux, though were confined on either side by minefields (some previously laid by the Canadians) so that their axis of advance was narrow. Morning fog and mist added to the initial confusion, as well as keeping British aircraft temporarily at bay. Finally breaking into

Two mobile Flak guns of the 12th SS-Panzer-Division "Hitlerjugend"pass through a Normandy town towards the front. The panzer-grenadierstanding on the right with his back to the camera has the deadly MG42 machine-gun slung over his right shoulder. (© US National Archives)

the open fields, 15th Scottish was beset by snipers, or by whom they took to be snipers, but were really diehard Hitlerjugend holding onto their positions. Infantrymen later described how their over-reactions to rifle-shots caused more chaos than the snipers themselves, as the British crisscrossed the sector with more fire than the Germans did. It took some time for VIII Corps to realize they hadn't just encountered an outpost line of 12th SS—it was their actual front line!

Meantime, Panzer Meyer had recognized the real British thrust and canceled his counterattacks against XXX Corps. Instead he ordered his Panther battalion to hurry back to hit the flank of 15th Scottish and its accompanying 31st Tank Brigade. Batteries of 88mm guns moved up from their prior positions at the Odon and began to lay down fire, as did Tigers of the 101st SS-Panzer Battalion, which had wanted to get a rest in corps reserve. Meyer also entreated 21st Panzer Division to lend strength on the other side of the incursion, and General Feuchtinger complied by dispatching a company of Mark IVs.

The Scottish Corridor

After stop-and-start work on the first day of the offensive, on June 27, 15th Scottish lunged again and reached an intact bridge over the Odon at Tournaville. 43rd Wessex Division was following, to mop up remaining pockets of resistance, and now tanks of the 11th Armoured were passed through to exploit the bridgehead. The British seized the high ground, Hill 112, on the German side of the Odon, from which Caen could be seen from one direction and the roads to Paris in another. A battalion of Argylls which crossed the river gallantly attacked through woods to the right to establish another bridgehead at Gavrus. The British advance could have easily been bolder, except for incredible congestion back at the village of Cheux, where tanks simply clogged the streets, and made funneling strength to the spearheads a trial.

Nevertheless, in what came to be known as the "Scottish Corridor," by June 28 the front of the SS Hitlerjugend had been breached, and VIII Corps had only the Orne River left to surmount. Once past the Orne, there were no more natural obstacles upon which the Germans could rally. It could have been a major breakthrough; but Operation *Epsom* had gotten underway just a few days too late.

On the evening of June 28, the advance elements of 1st SS Panzer Division, Leibstandarte Adolf Hitler, reported to I SS Panzer Corps headquarters. Already, a newly arrived battlegroup of 2nd SS Panzer Das Reich, after its tortuous journey from Toulouse, had emerged to attack VIII Corps' right flank, along with elements of Panzer Lehr. And worst of all for VIII Corps, the II SS-Panzer Corps, commanded by Paul Hausser, consisting of the 9th SS Hohenstaufen and 10th SS Frundsberg Divisions, had finally arrived in Normandy after its long trip from the east. The 12th SS Panzer Hitlerjugend had finally been joined by its parent divisions in the fight.

Ironically, due to British skill at defensive fighting, the newly arrived divisions made little headway against the corridor formed by *Epsom*. II SS Panzer Corps suffered significant losses, as did Das Reich's battlegroup, while trying to hammer in the incursion's right flank.

The British still retained a preponderance of tanks and artillery, together with uncontested air power, so that enemy breakthroughs, particularly in daylight, were nearly impossible to achieve.

Nevertheless, with counterattacks now coming in from every side, and new enemy divisions identified, on June 29 Second Army commander Miles Dempsey cautiously withdrew the advance elements of 11th Armoured from the east side of the Odon. The remaining infantry could no longer hold Hill 112, and the next day Montgomery shut down *Epsom* entirely. Word apparently didn't reach the brave Argylls in time, as they held on to their bridgehead at Gavrus till the last minute, suffering accordingly before their retreat.

The End of *Epsom*

One is entitled to wonder whether the inglorious conclusion of Operation *Epsom* was a case of the Allies being fooled by their own, usually superb, intelligence. Through Ultra, the cracking of the Germans' top-secret Enigma code, the Allies were privy to the plans and intentions of the German High Command. And with its newly arriving divisions, that High Command doubtless wished to crush VIII Corps with a massive counteroffensive. But by the end of June only the advance elements of 1st and 2nd SS Panzer Divisions and II SS Panzer Corps had reached Normandy. In particular, most of their tank strength and heavy artillery was still on the way. One can question whether Montgomery was overly cautious in calling off Operation *Epsom* so soon, temporarily confusing German High Command intentions with actual German capability.

By June 30 the operation had cost the British some 4,000 casualties (most of them from 15th Scottish) and the Germans about 3,000 (largely from Hitlerjugend); yet the battle had mainly been fought by British spearheads, not the full force they might have brought to bear. Nevertheless, Montgomery had achieved one major goal, which he especially claimed as a priority in his postwar writings: He had drawn the majority of German panzer strength onto the British sector of the Normandy front. This, he claimed with justification, helped to allow the Americans to achieve a breakthrough on their sector of the front, and eventually to decide the campaign in favor of the Allies.

| Afterword

The performance of the Waffen-SS in Normandy, until the very last days of June 1944, is basically the story of the 12th SS Panzer Division Hitlerjugend—a division of untried young men who had nevertheless been observing and absorbing reports of the war for years, and who had gained a fierce determination to do their part. This was not especially a German phenomenon, as the American 101st Airborne Division was similarly a formation of young volunteers who, once in combat, immediately established themselves as equal to their predecessors. The Canadian 3rd Division, for that matter, was of equal makeup as a volunteer unit—seeing combat in Normandy for the first time—and their initial battles with the Hitlerjugend still stand as the most ferocious face-to-face contests in the campaign.

That the key city of Caen remained in German hands at the end of June 1944, however, is attributable foremost to the young 12th SS Panzer Division, which stood off the Canadians, British, and finally an offensive led by the Scottish, until their High Command finally organized reinforcement. Never again in the war would they play such a vital role for the Third Reich, even as their initial baptism in fire continues to rouse respect.

In Normandy the fighting would only increase in intensity through July, as SS Hitlerjugend was joined by the full strength of the 1st and 2nd SS Panzer, the 9th and 10th SS Panzer, and the 17th SS Panzergrenadiers, as well as other capable divisions from the Wehrmacht. The Allies, too, continued their build-up, until one side or the other had to break.

Suffice to say that in June 1944, after the surprise of the initial invasion, both sides needed to feel their way through the crucible of confrontational battle. It is largely due to the novice youngsters on both sides that the campaign briefly became a stalemate. The following month of July would more posit main strength against main strength, no longer a matter of young soldiers simply dying to prove themselves in battle. The contest in Normandy would continue through the late days of August, and then onto fields closer to and including the Third Reich itself.

Further Reading

Beevor, Antony. *D-Day: The Battle for Normandy*. New York: Viking, 2009.

Buffetaut, Yves. *Casemate Illustrated: The 2nd SS Panzer Division Das Reich* (translated by H. McAdams). Havertown: Casemate, 2017.

English, John. *Surrender Invites Death: Fighting the Waffen SS in Normandy*. Mechanicsburg: Stackpole Books, 2011.

Fey, Will. *Armor Battles of the Waffen-SS 1943–45* (translated by H. Henschler). Manitoba, Winnipeg: J. J. Fedorowicz Publishing, 1990.

Hastings, Max. *Overlord: D-Day & the Battle for Normandy*. New York: Simon & Schuster, 1984.

Keegan, John. *Six Armies in Normandy*. New York: The Viking Press, 1982.

McKee, Alexander. *Caen: Anvil of Victory*. New York: St. Martin's Press, 1964.

Reynolds, Michael Frank. *Steel Inferno: I SS Panzer Corps in Normandy*. Kent: Spellmount, 1997.

Számvébér, Norbert. *Waffen-SS Armour in Normandy: The Combat History of SS-Panzer Regiment 12 and SS-Panzerjäger Abteilung 12, Normandy 1944*. Solihull: Helion, 2012.

Tucker-Jones, Anthony. *Images of War: Armoured Warfare and the Waffen-SS 1944–1945*. Barnsley: Pen and Sword, 2017.

Williamson, Gordon. *The Waffen-SS, Vols. 1 and 2*. Oxford: Osprey, 2003–2004.

Index

Numbers in *italics* refer to illustrations.

Amselgruber, SS-Untersturmführer Thomas, *28*
Ardenne Abbey, 70, 71
Artillery
Canadian, 73, 79
Pak 40, *8*, 43, 64

Bäderkele, Hauptman, *53*, *58*
Bartling, Karl, *71*
Bayerlein, General Fritz, 13, 61
Bayeux, 30, 55, 58, 61, 64, 71, 74, 91
Beauvais, 29, *29*, 106
Beck, Wilhelm, *45*
Bergerie Farm, 79
Bittrich, Obergruppenführer, 12
Blainville, 64
Blumentritt, Günther, 15, 18–21
Bolgk, SS-Hauptsturmführer, *53*
Boyle, Sergeant, 97
Bretteville-l'Orgueilleuse, 6,74,
British army units
I Corps, 30
XXX Corps, *7*, 30, 64, 103, 107, 118, 121, 122
1/7th Queen's Royal Regiment, 109
1st Rifle Brigade, 107
3rd Infantry Division, 30
4th County of London Yeomanry, 107, 111
7th Armoured Division, 30, 98, 107, 117, 118, 119
8th King's Royal Irish Hussars, 109
11th Armoured Division, 120
15th Scottish Division, 121
22nd Armoured Brigade, 107
26th Anti-Tank Battalion, 109
31st Tank Brigade, *111*, 122
69th Infantry Brigade, 86, 91
Bronay, 86

Caen, 1, 3, *7*, *11*, 22, 25, 30, *33*, 35, *45*, 47, 52, 54, 57–64, 66, 68, 70, 71, 74, 86, 99, 101, 107, 109, 118, 120, 122, 124
Calais, 6, 56
Canadian army units
1st Hussars, 91, 96–7
2nd Canadian Armoured Brigade, 71, 84
2nd Canadian Corps, 98
3rd Anti-Tank Regiment, 73
3rd Canadian Infantry Division, 79, 98
6th Armoured Regiment, 79, 91
7th Canadian Infantry Brigade, 73, 74, 79, 98
9th Canadian Infantry Brigade, 86
46 Royal Marine Commando, 86
Cameron Highlanders, 73, 79
Canadian Scottish Regiment, 79
Fort Garry Horse, 86
North Shore Regiment, 86
Nova Scotia Highlanders, 71
Queen's Own Regiment of Canada, 97
Queen's Own Rifles, 91, 97
Régiment de la Chaudière, 86
Regina Rifle Regiment, 74
Royal Winnipeg Rifles, 78
Cardonville, 75
Carentan, 6, 30, 47, 49, 99–101
Carpiquet aerodrome, 70
Châtellerault, 47
Cheux, 74, 84, 86, 91, 121, 122
Churchill tanks, 111
Colwell, Lieutenant-Colonel R.J., 91, 96
Courseulles-sur-Mer, 55
Cromwell tanks, 107

Dedow, Jochen, 69
Die Woche magazine, 65
Diekmann, SS-Sturmbannführer, 43
Dietrich, Sepp, 15, 52, 53, 62, 64, 66
Domfront, 41
Dreux, 67, 68

Ehrsam, Werner, *6*
Erskine, General, 116

Falaise pocket, 37, 60
Feuchtinger, Edgar, 61, 68, 122
Fick, SS-Standartenführer, 15
Fontenay-le-Pesnel, 86
Foster, Brigadier Harry, 79
Funk, Grenadier Otto, 65, 93
Fuss, SS-Untersturmführer, *53*

German armies
Army Group B, 19, 37, 41, 53, 56
Army Group G, 19
Seventh Army, 6, 19, 41, 64, 100, 118
Fifteenth Army, 6, 19, 120
Marine Group West, 19
Transmission service, *81*
German Heer (army) units
I Panzer Corps, 52–58
1st Panzer Division, *45*

2nd Panzer Division, 10, 11, 12, 20, *38*, 103, 117
6th Fallschirmjäger Regiment, 100
9th Panzer Division, 11, 14
11th Panzer Division, 10, 11, 13
21st Panzer Division, 11, 12, 14, 30, 53, 55, 56–8, 62, 67, 68, 73, 74, 91, 122
22nd Panzer Regiment, 68
26th Panzergrenadier Regiment, 74, 78
116th Panzer Division, 11
352nd Infantry Division, 41
716th Infantry Division, 57, 58, 78, 86
Kampfgruppe Weidinger, 25, 42
Panzer Group West, 9, 11, 20, 22, 53, 54, 91, 99, *118*
Panzer Lehr Division, 10, 11, 13, 53, 67, 74, 103, *117*
see also Waffen-SS units
Guderian, General Heinz, 12, 22, *36*

half-tracks
SdKfz 234, 84
SdKfz 250, *26–7, 76, 77*
SdKfz 251, 35, 36, 38, *42*, 45, 74, *78, 98, 100*
Harmel, Kommandeur, 42
Hausser, Commandant Paul, 14, 118, 122
Heydte, Friedrich von der, 100
Hill 112, 122, 123
Himmler, Heinrich, 19
Hitler, Adolf, 33, *36*, 66
Hiwis, 42, 47, 58

Juno Beach, 55

Kharkov, battle of, 37
Krämer, SS-Brigadeführer Fritz, 57, 58, 62, 101
Krause, Sturmbannführer Bernhard, 74
Kübelwagens, *78*
Kursk, battle of, 9, 37, 108

La Flèche, 49
Lammerding, SS-Brigadeführer, *36*
Le Mans, 20, 41, 49
Le Mesnil-Patry, *6*, 78, 84, 91, 93, 97–8
Lion-sur-Mer, 62
Lisieux, 68
Luftwaffe 19, 20, 33, 61

Mailly-le-Camp, 29, 43
Maquis, 43
Marks, Major, 96, 97
Meyer, Hubert, 75
Meyer, Kurt, 21, 45, 60–74
Mirebeau, 49
Montgomery, General Bernard, 30, 84, 118, 120, 123
Mortain, 24, 36, 37, 41
Mue river, 75
Mue valley, 86

Normandy, battle of, 8, *10*, *15*, 24, 32, 43, 54, 64, 119
Norrey-en-Bessin, *6*, 74, 84, 91, 98,
North Africa, 54–6, 107, 120

Oberbefehlshaber West (OB West), 15, 19, 20, 22, 37
Oberkommando der Wehrmacht (OKW), 10, 19, 20, 52
Oldebroek, 32
Omaha Beach, 61, 99
Opel cars, 17
Operation Cobra, 47
Operation Epsom, 5, 7, 42, 44, *111*, 120, *121*–3
Operation Goodwood, 36
Operation Lüttich, 24, 37
Oppeln, Oberst von, 68
Oradour-sur-Glane, 43
Orne, 30, 58, 64, 74, 122
Ostendorf, SS-Brigadeführer, 15

Paderborn, 32
Panther tanks
12th SS Panzer Regiment, 23, *24, 40, 46,* 51, *52*, 70, *72, 79*
medium, 34–40, 82–8, 94
no. 219, *13, 83*
no. 313, *96*
no. 318, *7*
Panzer IV tanks
1st SS Panzer Regiment, *7, 12, 13, 33, 40,* 50, *94*
2nd SS Panzer Regiment, *19, 34, 39*, 50, *89, 94*
12th SS Panzer Division, *6, 8, 9*, 10, 11, 13, 15, *16, 20,* 25, 44, *45*, 55–5, 62-9, 74–7, 84–6, 91–99, 103, 124
12th SS Panzer Regiment, 23, 24, *40, 46*, 70, *72*
medium, 34, 94
no. 536 (Kretschmar's), 80
Pemsel, General, 100
Philipsen, SS-Obersturmführer Hannes, 119
Poitiers, 47
postcards: Hitler Youth, 92
Prinz, Karl-Heinz, *71*
prisoners of war, *81*
Putot, 6, 74, 78–9, 84, 98

Rasch, Hanno, *29*
Rommel, Field Marshal Erwin, *15*, 19, 22, 53–6, 74, 118
Rots, 86
Rundstedt, Field Marshal Gerd von, 15, 18–9, 22, 54, *61*, 66

Saint-Lô, 47, 49
Saumur, 47
Schweppenburg, Leo Geyr von, 22
  criticisms of I Panzer Corps, 52–8
  profile, 22
  report, 8, 15, 55
Schwimmwagens, *57, 114*
Sherman tanks, *63*, 70-5, 79, 86, 91, 96–7, *102*, 107, 111, *113*, 116
Siebken, Sturmbannführer, 78
Simonds, General, 98
Stahl, Theo, *69*
StuG III tanks, 35, 37-8, 41, 43, 49, *64*
StuG IV tanks, *77*
Stuttgarter Illustrierte, *93*

Thury-Harcourt bridge, 57, 61
Tiger tanks
  no. 009, *48*
  no. 12, *113*, 116
  no. 101, *114*
  no. 112 (Ernst's), *115*, 116, *117*
  no. 131, *109*
  no. 211, *31, 32*
  no. 221, *113*
  no. 231, *105, 112*
  no. 232, *105, 112*
  no. 311, *101*
  no. 323 (Berhausen's), *99*
  no. 331, *28, 102*
  no. 334, *105*
  SS Heavy Panzer Battalion, *25*
  Tiger I, *103*
  Warmbrunn's, *112*
Tilly-sur-Seulle, 103, *105*
Todt organization, 58
Toulouse, 38, 41, 122
Tulle, 43

Uphoff, SS-Untersturmführer, *55*
Urbanitz, SS-Sturmbannführer Erich, *71*
US army units
  101st Airborne Division, 4

Villers-Bocage, battle of, *6*, 29, 30, *100*, *105*, 107, *108*, 109, 111, *113, 115–9*

Waffen-SS
  efficiency, 10
  fighting qualities, 8
Waffen-SS units
  I SS Panzer Corps, 99, 101, 103, 107
  II SS Panzer Corps, 32, 42, 44, 118
  1st SS Panzer Division Leibstandarte Adolf Hitler, *7*, 10, *12*, 20, 33, *35*, *45*, 50, *82*, *90*, 108, 122
  1st SS Panzergrenadier Regiment, 35
  2nd SS Panzer Division Das Reich, 25, 37, 41, 50
  2nd SS Panzer Regiment, *19, 34, 39*, 50, *89, 94*
  2nd SS Panzergrenadier Regiment, 50
  3rd SS Panzergrenadier Regiment, 50
  4th SS Panzergrenadier Regiment, 50
  9th SS Panzer Division Hohenstaufen, 10, *40*, 42, 43, 50
  10th SS Artillery Regiment, *44*
  10th SS Panzer Division, 11, 15, 25, 32
  10th SS Panzer Division Frundsberg, 32, 43, 51
  10th SS Panzer Regiment, *34*, 43, 51, *88*
  12th SS Panzer Division, *9*, 10-16, *45*, 55, 62, *67-9*, 77, 86, 91, 97–8, 103
  12th SS Panzer Division Hitlerjugend, *6*, *8* 10, *17*, *20*, 25, 44, 51, 53, *54*, 62, 68, 74, 75, 84, *85*, 91, 96, 98–9, 124
  12th SS Panzer Regiment, 79
  17th SS Panzer Reconnaissance Battalion, 49
  17th SS Panzergrenadier Division Götz von Berlichingen, 10, 25, 47, 51, 99
  17th SS Panzerjäger, 25, 47
  21st SS Panzergrenadier Regiment, 44, 51
  25th SS Panzergrenadier Regiment, *11*, *21*, 51, 60, 71, 74
  26th SS Panzer Regiment, 74
  101st SS Heavy Panzer Battalion, *6*, *10*, 25, *29*, 99, *100*, 101, 103, *106*, 108, *116*, 119
  102nd SS Heavy Panzer Battalion, 32
  see also German Heer (army) units
war crimes, 43, 66, 71
Westernhagen, SS-Sturmbannführer Heinz von, 29, 101
Wildgoose, Captain, 96
Witt, SS-Gruppenführer Fritz, 60, 62, 68, *73*
Wittmann, SS-Obersturmführer Michael, 104, 108, *109–10*, 111, 117, 118
Woll, SS-Unterscharführer Bobby, *110*
Wünsche, Max, *44*, 45, 70
Wyman, Brigadier R.A., 91